W9-CYD-144

# BEYOND BOUNDARIES

## PARTICIPANT'S GUIDE

## Other Resources by John Townsend

*Now What Do I Do?*
*Who's Pushing Your Buttons?*

## With Henry Cloud

*Boundaries*
*Boundaries Workbook*
*Boundaries audio*
*Boundaries video curriculum*
*Boundaries Face to Face*
*Boundaries Face to Face audio*
*Boundaries in Dating*
*Boundaries in Dating Workbook*
*Boundaries in Dating audio*
*Boundaries in Dating curriculum*
*Boundaries in Marriage*
*Boundaries in Marriage Workbook*
*Boundaries in Marriage audio*
*Boundaries in Marriage curriculum*
*Boundaries with Kids*
*Boundaries with Kids Workbook*
*Boundaries with Kids audio*
*Boundaries with Kids curriculum*
*How People Grow*
*How People Grow Workbook*
*How People Grow audio*
*Making Small Groups Work*
*Making Small Groups Work audio*
*The Mom Factor*
*Raising Great Kids*
*Raising Great Kids for Parents of Preschoolers curriculum*
*Raising Great Kids Workbook for Parents of Preschoolers*
*Raising Great Kids Workbook for Parents of School-Age Children*
*Raising Great Kids Workbook for Parents of Teenagers*
*Raising Great Kids Audio Pages®*
*Safe People*
*Safe People Workbook*
*12 "Christian" Beliefs That Can Drive You Crazy*

LEARNING TO TRUST AGAIN IN RELATIONSHIPS

# BEYOND BOUNDARIES

## PARTICIPANT'S GUIDE
### SIX SESSIONS

# DR. JOHN TOWNSEND
with Christine M. Anderson

ZONDERVAN®

ZONDERVAN.com/
AUTHORTRACKER
follow your favorite authors

ZONDERVAN

*Beyond Boundaries Participant's Guide*
Copyright © 2011 by Dr. John Townsend

This title is also available as a Zondervan ebook.
Visit www.zondervan.com/ebooks.

Requests for information should be addressed to:

Zondervan, Grand Rapids, Michigan 49530

ISBN 978-0-310-68447-3

Published in association with Yates & Yates, www.yates2.com.

*Cover design: Extra Credit Projects*
*Cover photography: GettyImages®*
*Interior design: Matthew Van Zomeren*

*Printed in the United States of America*

15  16  17  18  /QG/  22  21  20  19  18  17  16  15  14  13  12  11  10  9  8  7  6  5  4  3  2  1

# Contents

# About the Study

Your life is ultimately about relationship. More than anything in the world, you are meant to connect and relate in deep, meaningful, and positive relationships—with both God and people. The challenge comes when your significant relationships become unhealthy or even toxic ...

- A good friend repeatedly betrays your confidence.
- Your business partner lies about finances and you nearly lose your business.
- A parent with personal problems takes it out on you.
- The person you're dating or married to becomes harsh and controlling.
- Someone you care about has an addiction and abandons the relationship.

At such times, it's essential to establish healthy relational boundaries to protect yourself. But after a season of withdrawal and self-protection, your desire to connect will return. You want to begin again—in a new or existing relationship—but your trust muscle has been damaged. Now the questions become, *How do I know if I'm ready? When is it safe to take a risk with someone? How do I learn to trust again?*

These are the kinds of questions *Beyond Boundaries* addresses. It's designed to teach you how to identify and grow from whatever went wrong in your relationship, help you to

7

determine if someone is worthy of your trust now, and show you how to manage the process of opening up in a gradual and safe way.

As good as that sounds, it could be that you still have concerns. You're not sure you want to even talk about trusting again let alone take steps to let someone into your life. You might relate to one of these concerns ...

- *I don't want to seem like a victim.* You are probably a busy, active person with lots of strengths, but that doesn't negate the fact that strong people can be wounded too. Acknowledging the fallout of your difficult relationships does not mean you are weak, powerless, or a whiner.

- *I'm not ready for anything that pushes me to be vulnerable.* It's impossible to be vulnerable and learn the skills in *Beyond Boundaries* if you feel pressured or feel that you don't have a choice. It is always okay to say, "I'm not comfortable opening up," or "This is a bad time for me." Nothing in the curriculum is going to force you to talk about anything until you're ready.

- *My situation is deeply painful.* The deepest kind of injury you can experience is a relational injury because that's what matters the most. Nothing on the video or in this participant's guide will minimize, negate, or dismiss what you've experienced.

- *I don't want any simplistic formulas.* A one-size-fits-all approach doesn't help anyone. Your life and relationships are complex and this material takes that seriously.

I understand how hard it is to take the first steps in learning to trust again, but I promise you it's worth it. In fact, I have a challenge for you: Take more risks than you're comfortable with. The material provides opportunities for you to open up, learn what relationship is about, and develop deeper connections, but it only works as far as the risks you take. Don't play it safe. With every healthy risk, you'll gain more confidence, and the quality of the relationships you want to have will become significantly more fulfilling.

Whatever your loss or whatever your concern, you are designed to live in relationship, to reconnect, and to be vulnerable. Your difficulties can be redeemed and your self-protection resolved if you move into the right paths. Intimacy is complex, but it's not mysterious. Just as the laws of boundaries are clear, so are the rules of closeness and risk. You were made to live beyond self-protection and to be close to other people. You were meant to be free, not careful; open about yourself, not closed down; capable of deep attachments, not disconnected. You were designed to follow love and live in love, becoming like the One who embodies love itself. And that is my prayer for you.

The work and the risks are worth it. May you find the life that God intended for you in the journey.

*Dr. John Townsend*

# How to Use This Guide

### Group Size

The *Beyond Boundaries* video curriculum is designed to be experienced in a group setting such as a Bible study, Sunday school class, or any small group gathering. To ensure everyone has enough time to participate in discussions, it is recommended that large groups break up into smaller groups of four to six people each.

### Materials Needed

Each participant should have his or her own participant's guide, which includes note-taking outlines for video segments, directions for activities and discussion questions, as well as personal studies to deepen learning between sessions.

### Timing

The time notations—for example (17 minutes)—indicate the *actual* time of video segments and the *suggested* times for each activity or discussion. For example:

**Individual Activity:** **What I Want to Remember** (2 minutes)

Adhering to the suggested times will enable you to complete each session in one hour. If you have a longer meeting, you may wish to allow more time for discussion and activities. You may also opt to devote two meetings rather than one to each session. In addition to allowing discussions to be more spacious, this has the added advantage of allowing group members to read related chapters in the *Beyond Boundaries* book and to complete the personal study between meetings. In the second meeting, devote the time allotted for watching the video to discussing group members' insights and questions from their reading and personal study.

## Facilitation

Each group should appoint a facilitator who is responsible for starting the video and for keeping track of time during discussions and activities. Facilitators may also read questions aloud and monitor discussions, prompting participants to respond and assuring that everyone has the opportunity to participate.

## Personal Studies

Maximize the impact of the curriculum with additional study between group sessions. Every personal study includes reflection questions, Bible study, and a guided prayer activity. You'll get the most out of the curriculum by setting aside about one hour between sessions for personal study. For each session, you may wish to complete the personal study all in one sitting or to spread it out over a few days.

# Understanding the Problem
## RECLAIMING TRUST

Why hadn't I seen that the price of being *safe*—is the cost of being *solitary*? Why hadn't I seen that distrust can destroy a life?

Ann Voskamp, *A Holy Experience* blog post

## Welcome!

Welcome to Session 1 of *Beyond Boundaries*. If this is your first time together as a group, take a moment to introduce yourselves to each other before watching the video. Then let's get started!

## Video: Understanding the Problem (18 minutes)

Play the video segment for Session 1. As you watch, use the accompanying outline (pages 14–16) to follow along or to take notes on anything that stands out to you.

### Notes

We can live an island-like existence, but God did not design life this way. We were meant to be connected and in relationship.

God never designed us to live like an island forever—protected and guarded and safe.

We can move beyond isolation and withdrawal—even when there's been a lot of damage—and move back into intimacy and vulnerability the way that God intended.

Four sequential events:

1. We were designed for relationship.

   Vertical relationship with God (Psalm 42:1)


   Horizontal relationship with others (Ecclesiastes 4:9)


2. There is damage.

   We are not good to each other (Genesis 3).


   Functional trust: You trust someone because they are dependable.

   Relational trust: You know all of me and still accept me; you're safe.


3. We need boundaries.

   Boundaries help us when a relationship is difficult.


   Let your yes be yes and your no be no (Matthew 5:37).


   Defining boundary: Your values, beliefs, and what you stand for

Protective boundary: Protects you from harm

4. We experience the return of desire.

We are relational beings.

Double-bind: We need relationship and we fear relationship.

*Beyond Boundaries* is about learning when it's safe to trust again and how to open up to the right sorts of people.

Action steps

1. Admit to someone you trust that you might not want to move beyond boundaries.

2. Write down two protective boundaries and two defining boundaries you have.

3. Ask God to prepare your heart to move toward vulnerability and intimacy again.

**Group Discussion** (40 minutes)

Take a few minutes to talk about what you just watched.

1. What part of the teaching had the most impact on you?

### Designed for Relationship

2. God created us with a desire for connection so we would be drawn into deep and life-giving relationships—with him and with other people. The psalmist describes his draw to relationship with God as an intense thirst: "As the deer pants for streams of water, so my soul pants for you, my God" (Psalm 42:1).

   • How do you experience your desire for relationship with God? In other words, what makes you aware of your need for God and of your desire to be closer to him?

   • Similarly, how do you experience your desire for relationship with others (family, friends, a spouse, etc.)? What makes you aware of your need to be with others and of your desire for strong and authentic relationships?

   • What similarities or differences do you notice between your desire for connection with God and your desire for connection with others? For example, is one desire

17

stronger or more frequent than the other? Easier to recognize? Harder to act on or experience?

3. On the video, John uses an island to describe how boundaries keep us safe for a time but can also cut us off from developing trusting relationships. Using the same analogy, imagine there is a sign posted on buoys off the coast of your island. Which of the phrases below comes closest to describing what the sign might say?

☐ *No access*: I pretty much hold everyone at arm's length in one way or another.

☐ *Restricted access*: I rarely entrust myself to others. If I do allow someone into my life, it's typically on a temporary basis.

☐ *Guarded access*: I trust and connect with a few people, but I'm cautious about allowing new people into my life.

☐ *Fair access*: I have long-term and trusting connections with others and am generally open to allowing new people into my life.

☐ *Open access*: I work to strengthen connections in my existing relationships and actively seek out new relationships.

☐ Other:

Overall, how have difficult relationships influenced your "access"—the degree to which you are accessible or open to connecting with and trusting others?

## *Damage and Boundaries*

4. When relational trust is damaged, it changes the way we experience life. Which of the following common responses to loss of trust do you relate to most? If you feel comfortable, share an experience that illustrates your response.

   ☐ *Withdrawal*: I become careful, reserved, and avoid situations in which I might feel vulnerable.

   ☐ *Movement to task*: I overinvest in tasks related to work, career, school, activities, hobbies, or service.

   ☐ *Unbalanced "giver" relationships*: I become the "giver" in my relationships to avoid being the "receiver."

   ☐ *Bad habits*: I develop a troublesome behavior pattern, such as eating or sleep problems, obsessive behavior, or an addiction.

   ☐ Other:

5. We establish protective boundaries in relationships to separate ourselves from people who have harmed us. Sometimes those boundaries are formal and clearly articulated to the other person; and other times they may be informal or unspoken, such as emotional withdrawal.

   • Protective boundaries that are clearly articulated to another person include statements like these:

     *If you continue being thirty minutes late to events, I will take a separate car.*

     *I need a better work ethic from you in the office or we'll have to make some changes.*

     *If you won't stop drinking too much, I will take the kids and move out.*

     *I want to see my grandkids at times when you don't need a babysitter; otherwise, I feel taken advantage of.*

Have you ever had to establish this kind of protective boundary with someone? Or has someone else ever set this kind of boundary with you? Briefly describe the situation and the impact the boundary had on you.

- Protective boundaries that are informal or unspoken might include such things as:

    *Emotional withdrawal or distancing*

    *Choosing not to talk about certain topics*

    *Limited interest in new relationships*

    *Unwillingness to be vulnerable*

    *Maintaining a pleasant relationship rather than a close relationship*

    *Little demonstrated desire for connection or emotional intimacy*

    How have you experienced this kind of boundary, either in yourself or in someone close to you?

## The Return of Desire

6. We need relationship and yet we also fear relationship. It's not uncommon to feel pulled back and forth between the two desires—one says, "I want to get closer," and the other says, "Warning, danger!" Generally speaking, which

20

are you more aware of in your life right now—your desire for relationship or your fear of relationship? Why?

7. *Beyond Boundaries* is about taking relational risks and learning how to trust again. Which number on the continuum below best describes how you feel about exploring these issues?

| 1 2 | 3 4 | 5 6 | 7 | 8 9 10 |
|---|---|---|---|---|
| I feel guarded and cautious. | | I feel mixed— part of me feels guarded and part of me feels excited. | | I feel excited and eager to begin. |

8. As you work through the six sessions of this curriculum together, what do you need or want from the other members of the group? Use one or more of the sentence starters below, or your own statement, to help the group understand the best way to companion you. As each person responds, use the chart on pages 22–23 to briefly note what is important to that person and how you can be a good companion to them.

*It really helps me when ...*

*I tend to withdraw when ...*

*I'll know this group is a safe place if you ...*

*In our discussions, the best thing you could do for me is ...*

| NAME | THE BEST WAY I CAN BE A GOOD COMPANION FOR THIS PERSON |
|---|---|
|  |  |
|  |  |
|  |  |
|  |  |
|  |  |

**Individual Activity:** **What I Want to Remember** (2 minutes)

Complete this activity on your own.

1. Briefly review the outline and any notes you took.
2. In the space below, write down the most significant thing you gained in this session—from the teaching, activities, or discussions.

   *What I want to remember from this session ...*

## Closing Prayer

Close your time together with prayer.

## SESSION 1 PERSONAL STUDY

### Read and Learn

Read chapters 1–4 of *Beyond Boundaries*. Use the space below to note any insights or questions you want to bring to the next group session.

### Study and Reflect

1. In which of your relationships do you currently have some kind of protective boundary (formal or informal) to guard your heart and help you feel safe? Check all that apply.

☐ Parents

☐ Siblings

☐ Extended family members

☐ Spouse (current or former)

☐ Children

☐ Dating relationships

☐ People at church

☐ Friends

☐ Colleagues

☐ New people or people in general

☐ Other:

Generally speaking, what kinds of things caused you to establish boundaries in these relationships?

How have these boundaries been beneficial and served you well?

What have these boundaries cost you, or in what ways might they no longer be serving you well?

2. To better understand the differences between defining boundaries and protective boundaries, read "Two Kinds of Boundaries" on pages 26–28. Then use the charts on pages 29–30 to identify some of your defining boundaries and protective boundaries and how you have acted on both kinds of boundaries recently.

## TWO KINDS OF BOUNDARIES

It's important to understand that there are two types of boundaries — defining boundaries and protective boundaries.

*Defining boundaries* are values that establish who you are and who you are not. They are at the core of your identity and reflect what you believe is important and valuable in life. Here are a few examples:

- I follow God and his ways and will always live my life in him.

- I love my family and friends, and I will treat them with grace and truth.
- I say and receive the truth; I'm neither silent in saying it nor defensive in receiving it.

These defining boundaries help you and others know the real you, the person who has substance and stands for things that matter. They help guide your decisions and directions in life.

Here are some examples of how defining boundaries might be used in your relationships:

- "I'm looking for a position that fits my strategic abilities rather than one that is in operations."
- "We have a rule that all who live in this house go to church."
- "I want to hear the truth from you about how you think we are doing in our relationship."
- "I'm a night owl, so let's not plan something that requires that we get up at O'dark-thirty."

This is simply how you tell people who you are and how they tell you who they are. You clarify and define yourselves with these sorts of boundaries.

*Protective boundaries* are different. They are designed to "guard your heart" (Proverbs 4:23) and your life from danger or trouble. There are times when you must protect your values, emotions, gifts, time, and energy from people and situations that may waste or injure them.

A protective boundary might begin with a statement like this: "I want us to work this out, but nothing I've said has made any difference, so I'm taking a different route." The consequences portion of the boundary then needs to be stated in an "If ... then ..." form to make sure the other person understands you mean business. For example:

27

- "If you continue being thirty minutes late to events, I will take a separate car."
- "I need a better work ethic from you in the office or we'll have to make some changes."
- "If you won't stop drinking too much or using drugs, I will take the kids and move out."

Here's the important distinction between a defining boundary and a protective boundary. A defining boundary is forever and unchangeable, part of what makes you "you"; a protective boundary can change if the other person responds to it in a healthy way.

*Beyond Boundaries*, pages 38–40

| DEFINING BOUNDARY | HOW I HAVE ACTED ON THIS BOUNDARY RECENTLY |
|---|---|
| My kids are my first priority. | I rescheduled a work trip so I could attend Bella's choir concert. |
| I will always tell the truth. | I acknowledged the error in the report as my mistake rather than making excuses or blaming someone else. |
| I come alive when I am with lots of people in a high-energy environment. | I decided to apply for a summer job at the outdoor amusement park rather than for one at the public library. |
|  |  |
|  |  |
|  |  |
|  |  |
|  |  |

| PROTECTIVE BOUNDARY | HOW I HAVE ACTED ON THIS BOUNDARY RECENTLY |
|---|---|
| I keep things pleasant but emotionally distant with my parents. | During our last visit, I avoided talking about topics that might make me feel vulnerable. |
| I tend to be suspicious of new people rather than giving them the benefit of the doubt. | I cut short a conversation with a new person at work because I didn't feel comfortable telling her about myself so soon. |
| I won't allow my friend Jim to keep taking advantage of me financially. | I told him, "I won't lend you any more money until I see you making serious efforts to find a job." |
| | |
| | |
| | |
| | |
| | |

- Briefly review the defining boundaries you wrote on your chart on page 29. Which one would you say is your greatest asset or strength in relationships? In other words, which one tends to consistently draw you closer to others?

- Briefly review your protective boundaries in the chart on page 30. Which one is or has been most important in providing you a sense of emotional safety and protection?

- What parallels or contradictions do you notice between your most important *defining* boundary (the one you identified as your greatest asset in relationships) and your most important *protective* boundary? For example, if a commitment to always tell the truth is your strongest defining boundary, how is telling the truth evident or absent in your most important protective boundary?

3. When you think about moving beyond boundaries and learning to trust again, what relationships come to mind? (You may wish to review the boxes you checked in response to question 1, page 25). Use the chart on page 33 to write down any names you think of. If you also have difficulty trusting new people or people in general, write that on the chart as well. Note that in writing down someone's name, you aren't making any decisions or commitments about choosing to trust this person again. You are simply identifying relationships in which you have a boundary because trust has been damaged. Once you've written down the names, briefly assess your current level of trust for each one using the following scale:

3 = I have some trust
2 = I have limited trust
1 = I have very little trust
0 = I have zero trust

## UNDERSTANDING THE PROBLEM

| NAME | MY CURRENT LEVEL OF TRUST |
|------|---------------------------|
|      |                           |
|      |                           |
|      |                           |
|      |                           |
|      |                           |
|      |                           |
|      |                           |
|      |                           |
|      |                           |
|      |                           |

As you review the names you wrote on the chart on page 33, what emotions are you aware of? For example: fear, excitement, resistance, dread, anticipation, or something else?

In which relationship, if any, do you feel most drawn to reestablishing trust or to developing a deeper connection?

How do you hope this relationship might be different than it is now?

4. Choosing to trust someone requires taking a risk and stepping into unknown territory. In the midst of all we do not know when we take a risk with another person, God invites us to throw the full weight of our trust on him. As you read the following verses, underline the images used to describe God's trustworthiness.

> The LORD is my strength and my shield; my heart trusts in him, and he helps me.　　　　*Psalm 28:7a*

This I declare about the LORD: He alone is my refuge, my place of safety; he is my God, and I trust him.

*Psalm 91:2 NLT*

Those who trust in the LORD are like Mount Zion, which cannot be shaken but endures forever.

*Psalm 125:1*

Trust in the LORD forever, for the LORD, the LORD himself, is the Rock eternal. *Isaiah 26:4*

I have come as a light to shine in this dark world, so that all who put their trust in me will no longer remain in the dark. *John 12:46 NLT*

Christ will make his home in your hearts as you trust in him. Your roots will grow down into God's love and keep you strong. *Ephesians 3:17 NLT*

Of the images you underlined, which one resonates most with you?

In what ways, if any, does this image of God's trustworthiness encourage or reassure you about potentially taking a risk to trust other people in your life?

## Guided Prayer

*God, thank you for creating me with a desire for relationship—with you and with other people. I believe my relationships have the potential for many good things I want and need.*

*Even so, I feel caught in the double-bind of both wanting and fearing closer relationships. The possibility of opening myself up to new people or to someone who has hurt me brings up all kinds of things—thoughts, concerns, emotions, questions. Right now, I am especially aware of ...*

*More than anything, I need your help with ...*

*Give me wisdom as I discern the people you are leading me to consider trusting again or to trusting for the first time. Particularly, I need your wisdom about ...*

*Please prepare my heart to be open to what you have to teach me and to begin to move toward risk again. I ask for courage to surrender my resistance to you, especially my resistance to ...*

*Thank you for being a place of safety for me and a rock I can rely on as I learn to trust again. Amen.*

# Knowing When You're Ready, Part 1
## UNLEARNING OLD WAYS

We must always be ready to come out into the open.
Dietrich Bonhoeffer, *The Cost of Discipleship*

**Group Discussion:** **Checking In** (5 minutes)

Welcome to Session 2 of *Beyond Boundaries*. A key part of getting to know God better is sharing your journey with others. Before watching the video, briefly check in with each other about your experience since the last session. For example:

- How did the last session impact you, your relationships with others, or your relationship with God?
- What insights did you discover in the personal study or in the chapters you read from the *Beyond Boundaries* book?
- What questions would you like to ask the other members of your group?

**Video:** **Knowing When You're Ready, Part 1** (16 minutes)

Play the video segment for Session 2. As you watch, use the accompanying outline (pages 38–41) to follow along or to take notes on anything that stands out to you.

*Notes*

There are rules of preparation for moving beyond boundaries.

Four keys in knowing how to be ready for a good relationship:

1. Admit you were hurt and receive support.

38

Jesus modeled vulnerability: "My soul is overwhelmed with sorrow to the point of death. Stay here and keep watch with me" (Matthew 26:38).

2. Understand your past choices.

This isn't about blaming or judging. It's about taking responsibility.

If you don't take responsibility for what you were doing when you chose that person, you're vulnerable to making that same mistake again.

We choose people for a "payoff."

3. Connect the dots to your past.

Every relationship problem has a "parent," and that parent is the past. Somewhere in the past is an older relationship that has affected the people we've chosen.

Wisdom has been defined as "skill in living." This is key for understanding your past.

39

"These are the proverbs of Solomon, David's son, king of Israel. Their purpose is to teach people wisdom and discipline, to help them understand the insights of the wise. Their purpose is to teach people to live disciplined and successful lives, to help them do what is right, just, and fair" (Proverbs 1:1–3 NLT).

4. Let go of the past.

This doesn't mean pretending it never happened.

We have to grieve it. Then we can redeem the relationship for something good in the future.

Letting go in grief is something God created for us; it's a blessing.

The Bible describes Jesus as a man of sorrows and well acquainted with grief (Isaiah 53:3).

40

Action steps

1. Check to see if you've skipped one of the steps.

2. Without shame or blame, connect the dots and say, "I chose that difficult relationship because I wanted _____. I wanted this payoff."

3. Allow yourself to experience grief in the company of another person—someone who is safe and who cares about you.

**Group Discussion** (37 minutes)

Take a few minutes to talk about what you just watched.

1. What part of the teaching had the most impact on you?

*Getting Ready for a Good Relationship*

2. Sometimes we jump the gun in our relational life by trusting too soon. Instead of moving in a "ready-aim-fire" sequence, our approach is more like "fire-fire-fire." Other times, we might be so mistrustful that we're prone to a "ready-ready-ready" or "never ready" approach. Or we

41

might swing back and forth from one extreme to the other. Generally speaking, how would you characterize your approach to trust in relationships?

3. What kinds of things *inside yourself* typically make you feel like you are ready to trust someone more? For example, do you have an instinct that this person is trustworthy, or move ahead on impulse?

### Admit the Hurt and Receive Support

4. Place an X on the continuum below to indicate how you tend to respond when you are wounded in a relationship.

It's difficult for me
to admit the hurt.
I do my best to remain
self-sufficient and
emotionally hidden.

I am able to
admit the hurt.
I allow myself to
receive support and
to be emotionally
vulnerable.

If you feel comfortable, briefly share an experience that illustrates your tendency.

5. Consider a positive experience you've had in receiving support from someone when you were hurting. What did this person do, or not do, that enabled you to receive their support? If you have difficulty recalling a positive experience,

what kinds of things would you hope someone would do, or not do, to support you when you are hurting?

### Understand Your Past Choices and Connect the Dots

6. A key piece of understanding past relational choices is identifying the payoff. The payoff is the benefit you hoped for when you began a relationship with someone. For example:

    *Warmth*: She was gentle and nurturing with me.

    *Affirmation*: He saw the good in me.

    *Safety*: He did not condemn or judge me.

    *Structure*: She was organized and got things done.

    *Humor*: She helped lighten the burdens and cheered me up.

    *A great family*: His relatives were much healthier than mine.

    *Drive*: She was focused and knew where she was going.

    *Initiative*: She took risks and was brave in making decisions.

    *Competency*: He was talented, and I needed his talent in my organization.

    *People skills*: He handled people better than I did, so I depended on him.

    *Intelligence*: She was smart, and I needed smarts in my department.

    - When you consider a previous or current difficult relationship—with a family member, friend, colleague, spouse, or dating relationship—how would you describe the benefit you hoped for in that relationship?

- Because the need for this benefit was so strong, you may have minimized or denied something else in that person's character that ended up being a bigger deal than you originally thought. For example:

| | |
|---|---|
| deception | a victim stance |
| emotional unavailability | irresponsibility |
| control | distrust |
| manipulation | condemnation |
| excuses | self-absorption |
| blame | narcissism |

How would you describe what you may have minimized or denied about that person? How did you minimize or deny it?

7. On the video, John taught that we acquire wisdom when we study our past relational patterns and connect the dots to our current relational problems. Here is how King Solomon, the wisest man in the Bible, describes what is required to acquire wisdom:

Tune your ears to wisdom, and concentrate on understanding. Cry out for insight, and ask for understanding. Search for them as you would for silver; seek them like hidden treasures.       *Proverbs 2:2–4 NLT*

- Based on these verses, how would you describe the characteristics of someone who wants to acquire wisdom?

- What thoughts come to mind or what feelings are you aware of when you consider applying this same kind of intensity to seeking wisdom about your past relational patterns?

## Let Go of the Past

8. Letting go in grief is how we redeem a past relationship and make room for something good in the future. An essential part of grief is acknowledging that something we loved and valued is no more. It's not an easy thing to do and so it's natural that we might try to avoid it. Which of the following statements comes closest to describing any reasons you may have for avoiding grief?

☐ I avoid grief because I am afraid of how painful it will be.

☐ I avoid grief because I don't want to acknowledge—even to myself—how much I've lost.

☐ I avoid grief because I don't want to waste any more emotional energy on this person.

☐ I avoid grief because I feel like once it starts, it might never end.

☐ I'm not sure I avoid grief, but I don't seek it out either.

☐ Other:

In what ways, if any, do you think avoiding grief might have impacted you or made it difficult for you to move on to new or healthier relationships?

9. At the end of the group discussion for Session 1, you had the opportunity to share what you wanted or needed from the group and to write down the best way to companion each other (pages 22–23).

- Briefly restate what you asked for from the group in Session 1. What changes or clarifications would you like to make that would help the group know more about how to companion you well? As each person responds, add any additional information to the chart on pages 22–23. (If you were absent from the last session, share your response to question 8 on page 21. Then use the chart on pages 22–23 to write down what is important to each member of the group.)

- In what ways, if any, did you find yourself responding differently to other members of the group in this session based on what they asked for in the previous session? What made that easy or difficult for you to do?

**Individual Activity: What I Want to Remember** (2 minutes)

Complete this activity on your own.

1. Briefly review the outline and any notes you took.
2. In the space below, write down the most significant thing you gained in this session—from the teaching, activities, or discussions.

*What I want to remember from this session ...*

## Closing Prayer

Close your time together with prayer.

## SESSION 2 PERSONAL STUDY

**Read and Learn**

Read chapters 5–8 of *Beyond Boundaries*. Use the space below to note any insights or questions you want to bring to the next group session.

**Study and Reflect**

1. Briefly review the list of names you wrote on the chart in response to question 3 in the Session 1 personal study (page 32). These are the relationships in which you have a boundary because trust has been damaged. Choose one (two at most) to be your focus person for the remainder of this personal study. Write that person's name below.

2. On the video, John presented four steps that are essential preparation for moving beyond boundaries. Review the brief descriptions of the four steps below and circle the number on each continuum that best describes where you are with that step.

   *Admit the hurt and receive support.* I have told another human being the facts and feelings about what I experienced—how I was hurt and the impact it had on me. I have allowed myself to be vulnerable and to receive emotional support.

| 1 | 2 | 3 | 4 | 5 | 6 | 7 | 8 | 9 | 10 |
|---|---|---|---|---|---|---|---|---|----|

I have not taken this step. | I have stalled out or am still in process on this step. | I feel confident that I have worked through this step.

*Understand your past choices.* I have taken time to be a student of my relational choices. I can name the payoff I hoped for in my previous difficult relationship(s) and how I minimized or ignored reality in pursuit of that payoff.[1]

| 1 | 2 | 3 | 4 | 5 | 6 | 7 | 8 | 9 | 10 |
|---|---|---|---|---|---|---|---|---|----|

I have not taken this step. | I have stalled out or am still in process on this step. | I feel confident that I have worked through this step.

*Connect the dots.* I can identify the family dynamics that shaped my early relationships and life experiences. I understand how these dynamics and my response to them have influenced my poor relational choices.

| 1 | 2 | 3 | 4 | 5 | 6 | 7 | 8 | 9 | 10 |
|---|---|---|---|---|---|---|---|---|----|

I have not taken this step. | I have stalled out or am still in process on this step. | I feel confident that I have worked through this step.

*Let go of the past.* I have acknowledged my attachment, what I valued, and what I lost in my difficult relationship(s). I have given myself time to feel sad about my loss and to receive comfort from others.

| 1 | 2 | 3 | 4 | 5 | 6 | 7 | 8 | 9 | 10 |
|---|---|---|---|---|---|---|---|---|----|

I have not taken this step. | I have stalled out or am still in process on this step. | I feel confident that I have worked through this step.

---

1. See question 6 on page 43 in the group discussion for a brief definition of relational payoff and a list of payoff examples.

Based on your responses on the four continuums, how would you describe your overall readiness to move beyond boundaries?

Which, if any, of the four steps would you still need to work through to be ready to move beyond boundaries with your focus person?

## ADDITIONAL GUIDANCE TO HELP YOU GET READY

As you assessed your readiness on the continuums in question 2, you may have discovered an area in which you need help to take a next step. For additional guidance, see the following chapters in the *Beyond Boundaries* book:

Chapter 5: You Admit the Hurt and Receive Support (pages 61–66)

Chapter 6: You Understand Your Own Past Choices (pages 67–75)

Chapter 7: You Connect the Dots (pages 77–87)

Chapter 8: You Grieve and Let It Go (pages 89–102)

3. Connecting the dots can be one of the most challenging steps to complete. It focuses on identifying your family dynamics—the situations that shaped your early relationships and life experiences—and how your response to those dynamics has influenced your relational choices. To better understand this concept, read "What's Your Relational Narrative?" on pages 53–55.

Based on the examples of family dynamics you just read, how would you describe some of the family dynamics that characterized the home you grew up in? Write your responses on the chart on page 52. For each dynamic you write down, identify whether you responded with fusion or opposition and how your response has influenced your subsequent relational patterns. (If you have a hard time identifying your family dynamics but resonate with any of the examples you read about, use one or more of those examples as your starting point.)

| FAMILY DYNAMIC | FUSION OR OPPOSITION? | HOW MY RESPONSE HAS INFLUENCED MY RELATIONAL PATTERNS |
|---|---|---|
| My family was loving, but we almost never talked about negative emotions (anger, disappointment, fear, sadness). | Fusion | I have a hard time acknowledging problems in a relationship and tend to pick people who also have this issue. Even small problems often go unaddressed, get worse, and eventually undermine the relationship. |
|  |  |  |
|  |  |  |
|  |  |  |
|  |  |  |

Of the family dynamics and responses you identified, circle on the chart the one that may have had the strongest influence on the relationship with your focus person. Briefly describe below how you recognize this relational narrative in connection with your focus person.

## WHAT'S YOUR RELATIONAL NARRATIVE?

You may have heard that you become like those you are with and take on their characteristics. The psychological term for this is *fusion*. Fusion happens when an individual takes on the same problems experienced in his or her family. For example, an alcoholic family produces an alcoholic adult child. But there are also exceptions to this. Sometimes we react in *opposition* to the way we were treated in an effort to separate ourselves from the toxicity we experienced or because we are determined not to be like the people who wounded us. We react *against*. That's how the neat freak arises from the cluttered home and the rebel emerges from the overcontrolling environment.

On the next two pages are some examples of family dynamics and how a person might respond with either fusion or opposition. As you review the list, see if you resonate with any of these scenarios. Note that sometimes several patterns can be active simultaneously, so it's possible you could relate to more than one.

*(cont.)*

*Dynamic:* Your parents were nice people but discouraged honesty, confrontation, and anger.
*Fusion:* You avoid confrontation and often seem to find yourself with angry or controlling people.
*Opposition:* You become angry too quickly and are overly confrontational with others.

*Dynamic:* You experienced good structure and care in your family, but your family didn't talk about feelings or relational issues.
*Fusion:* You live in the world of the mind and are uncomfortable with the emotional side of life.
*Opposition:* You are so emotional that your feelings sometimes get you in trouble.

*Dynamic:* You had a parent who was loving but irresponsible or unreliable.
*Fusion:* You have difficulty taking responsibility for your life and give control of it to others.
*Opposition:* You had to grow up quickly and became overly responsible and guilt-ridden.

*Dynamic:* You had chaos in your home.
*Fusion:* You find yourself unable to meet goals, finish projects, and have structure in your life.
*Opposition:* You have become rigid and let your schedule get in the way of relationships.

*Dynamic:* You had an immature parent.
*Fusion:* You feel and sometimes act like a kid around other adults.
*Opposition:* You became what psychologists call the "parentified child." You learned to parent your parents by

taking care of their emotional needs, not being a bother, and always making them proud.

*Dynamic:* You had perfectionistic parents.
*Fusion:* You developed a false and ideal presentation of who you are to avoid judgment and shame.
*Opposition:* You throw your values and standards to the wind and give up trying to be a good person, knowing you will never be good enough.

Connecting your past to your present is an important part of moving beyond boundaries. When you identify your narrative—the situation that shaped your early relationships and life experiences—and understand your response to that narrative, you are well on your way to making sense of your past relational choices.

*Beyond Boundaries*, pages 80–83

4. Taking time to study your past relationships is an investment that promises a rich return of wisdom you can use in future relationships. The Bible has many things to say about wisdom—its purpose, where it comes from, its benefits and characteristics, who has it and who doesn't have it, how to get it, and more. Following are five passages that focus on wisdom. Read through the passages slowly and, if possible, out loud.

God gives out Wisdom free, is plainspoken in Knowledge and Understanding. He's a rich mine of Common Sense for those who live well, a personal bodyguard to the candid and sincere. He keeps his eye on all who live honestly, and pays special attention to his loyally committed ones. *Proverbs 2:6–8 MSG*

Wise choices will watch over you. Understanding will keep you safe. *Proverbs 2:11 NLT*

Don't turn your back on wisdom, for she will protect you. Love her, and she will guard you. Getting wisdom is the wisest thing you can do! And whatever else you do, develop good judgment. *Proverbs 4:6–7 NLT*

Wisdom and money can get you almost anything, but only wisdom can save your life.

*Ecclesiastes 7:12 NLT*

If any of you lacks wisdom, you should ask God, who gives generously to all without finding fault, and it will be given to you. *James 1:5*

- What do the passages reveal about God and wisdom?

- How would you describe the benefits of wisdom the passages present?

- Read through the passages again, underlining any words or phrases that stand out to you.

56

- What connections might you make between the words and phrases you underlined and your state of readiness to move beyond boundaries?

- How do you relate the truth of these passages to the relationship you have with your focus person?

5. What fears or resistance were you aware of in the process of completing this study?

What hopes or encouragement were stirred up in you?

## Guided Prayer

*God, thank you for providing boundaries I can use to guard my heart and keep myself safe. And thank you for teaching me how to be ready to move ahead when the need for boundaries has passed.*

*When I consider my past relational patterns, some things seem clear, but other things are hard to recognize or understand. Please open my eyes and help me to see what you see. I especially need help to see ...*

*I am encouraged by the promise that wisdom can protect me and that you are generous in giving wisdom to those who ask. I especially need your wisdom right now with ...*

*I know you understand all the hurt and history I have with my focus person. I need your guidance for my questions and confusion about this relationship, especially ...*

*Lord, I surrender everything I know and do not know about myself and my relationships to you. You know me better than I know myself—and what a grace that is! I believe you are at work in my life and I entrust myself to your love, to your guidance, and to your will for me this day. Amen.*

# Knowing When You're Ready, Part 2
## LEARNING NEW WAYS

God perceives the imperfections within us, and because of his love for us, urges us to grow up.

John of the Cross, *The Dark Night of the Soul*

## Group Discussion: Checking In (5 minutes)

Welcome to Session 3 of *Beyond Boundaries*. A key part of getting to know God better is sharing your journey with others. Before watching the video, briefly check in with each other about your experience since the last session. For example:

- How did the last session impact you, your relationships with others, or your relationship with God?
- What insights did you discover in the personal study or in the chapters you read from the *Beyond Boundaries* book?
- What questions would you like to ask the other members of your group?

## Video: Knowing When You're Ready, Part 2 (14 minutes)

Play the video segment for Session 3. As you watch, use the accompanying outline (pages 60–62) to follow along or to take notes on anything that stands out to you.

### Notes

This session is about learning new ways as you move forward into relationship.

1. Develop growth friendships.

- Let these relationships into your life at the same level of intimacy and vulnerability as your difficult relationship.

- Make sure these relationships are structured. They must include:
  Regularity
  Commitment
  Intentionality
  Focus

2. Learn to trust your defining boundaries.

The stronger your defining boundaries are, the less you are going to need protective boundaries.

People with defining boundaries aren't harsh or cold; they learn to speak the truth in love (Ephesians 4:15).

3. Let your values transform your desires.

Living out your values will change how you relate to people.

"Delight yourself in the LORD and he will give you the desires of your heart" (Psalm 37:4 NIV 1984).

4. Know which risks are worth taking and which are not.

- There is a difference between hurt and harm.

  "Above all else, guard your heart, for it is the wellspring of life" (Proverbs 4:23 NIV 1984).

- Does this relationship have some hurt to it or is it harming you? If there is harm, the risk might not be acceptable.

- What's the potential net result of the relationship? Is it worth the risk?

- Move past generalizations.

Action steps

1. Determine if you really have let your friends into your life at the same level as the difficult relationship.

2. Learn how to be around controlling people without feeling controlled.

3. Review how you may have confused hurt with harm.

62

**Group Discussion** (39 minutes)

Take a few minutes to talk about what you just watched.

1. What part of the teaching had the most impact on you?

*Develop Growth Relationships*

2. God often uses people—relationships—to provide for us and meet our needs.

   • Think back on the last day or two. In what ways, small or large, has God used your relationships to provide for you and to meet your needs?

   • If you suddenly lost one of these relationships, what kinds of needs in your life might no longer be met?

3. When we experience a relational injury, it takes another relationship to heal the injury. We must allow others—good people who care about us—to help us meet our needs. On the video, John described two essential requirements for these kinds of growth relationships. We must: (1) let these people in at the same level of intimacy and vulnerability of the difficult relationship; (2) establish a structure for the relationship that includes regularity, commitment, intentionality, and focus.

- Which of the two requirements do you think would be more challenging for you? Why?

- A wide range of people might be candidates for growth relationships—friends, small group members, mentors, spiritual directors, coaches, counselors, family members. What kind of person would you be most likely to seek out for a growth relationship? What qualities or characteristics in this person would be especially important to you?

## Learn to Trust Your Defining Boundaries

4. One of the most helpful things you can do to strengthen your defining boundaries is to make saying what is true and stating your opinion a routine part of your relationships. To what degree is this something you already practice in your relationships? Circle the number on the continuum below that best describes your response.

| 1 | 2 | 3 | 4 | 5 | 6 | 7 | 8 | 9 | 10 |
|---|---|---|---|---|---|---|---|---|---|

I almost never say what is true or state my opinion in relationships.

I sometimes say what is true and state my opinion in relationships.

I almost always say what is true and state my opinion in relationships.

- Now is your chance to practice saying what is true! If you feel comfortable doing so, share the number you circled and why you chose it.

- What unique challenges, if any, do you think people in your church or in the larger Christian community have when it comes to saying what is true, stating their opinions, and having strong defining boundaries?

5. People with strong defining boundaries are those who learn to speak the truth in love, a practice described in the apostle Paul's letter to the church at Ephesus.

> Speaking the truth in love, we will grow to become in every respect the mature body of him who is the head, that is, Christ.... Therefore each of you must put off falsehood and speak truthfully to your neighbor, for we are all members of one body. *Ephesians 4:15, 25*

In Greek, the phrase translated "speaking the truth" is one word, *alētheuō* (al-ayth-yoo´-o). It is a verb that might more literally be translated "truthing" or "truthspeaking."[2] The root of *alētheuō* includes the word *lēthō* (lay-tho), which can be translated "to conceal."[3] In Greek grammar, the prefix "a" functions as a negation of the word it precedes. So *alētheuō* (or *a-lētheuō*) can be understood to

---

2. A. Skevington Wood, "Ephesians," *The Expositor's Bible Commentary*, vol. 11, Frank E. Gaebelein, gen. ed. (Grand Rapids: Zondervan, 1978), 59.

3. Anthony C. Thiselton, "Truth," *New International Dictionary of New Testament Theology*, vol. 3, Colin Brown, gen. ed. (Grand Rapids: Zondervan, 1978, 1986), 884.

mean "*not* concealing" or the opposite of concealing. The gospel of Mark conveys this meaning when it describes the woman who touched Jesus and was healed from a flow of blood as one who told "the whole truth" (Mark 5:33).[4] She concealed nothing.

- How does this perspective on speaking the truth inform your understanding of what it means to have strong defining boundaries?

- What kinds of things within yourself typically make it difficult for you to tell someone the whole truth — about a situation, what you're feeling, your opinion, etc.?

- How do you understand the difference between merely speaking the truth and speaking the truth in love?

## *Let Your Values Transform Your Desires*

6. On the video, John told a story about a man who attended his twenty-year high school reunion and discovered he no longer felt any attraction to the woman he'd been crazy about at seventeen. Since high school, he had changed, his values had changed, and so his desires — what he wanted and was attracted to — had changed.

---

4. "Truth," 884.

66

- Overall, how would you describe the connections between your values, your desires, and your relationships right now? In what areas of your life do they strongly align or fail to align?

- What, if anything, do you wish were different about what you want from and what you are attracted to in other people?

7. You let your values transform your desires when you identify what is really important to you at the deepest level and then begin living out those values. This is part of what the apostle Paul meant when he wrote that it is possible to "be transformed by the renewing of your mind" (Romans 12:2).

- How do you respond to the idea that you can change whom you're attracted to—that you can increasingly find yourself drawn to better and healthier people? How confident are you that this is possible for you?

- When it comes to values, what do you struggle with more—knowing what is really important to you at the deepest level, or living out what's really important to you in your everyday life? Why do you think this is especially difficult for you?

67

## *Know Which Risks Are Worth Taking and Which Are Not*

8. When assessing acceptable and unacceptable risks in a relationship, we need to consider two questions:

   *Am I being hurt or harmed?* Hurt is the experience of something painful, but it may not be damaging. Harm creates significant problems, such as withdrawal from other relationships, personal decline, or diminished performance.

   *Is the relationship worth the time and energy I put into it?* Except for marriage, some relationships are worth it and some are not. Some may not produce enough good—increased love, connection, intimacy, trust—to be worth the investment of your limited time and energy.

   Which of these questions is most helpful to you in assessing acceptable and unacceptable risk in your difficult relationships? Why?

9. You're now at the halfway point in the curriculum. Take a few moments to reflect on what you've learned and experienced together so far and to talk about your hopes for the remainder of the course.

   • Since the first session, what shifts have you noticed in yourself in terms of how you relate to the group? For example, do you feel more or less guarded, more or less understood, more or less companioned, more or less connected, etc.?

- What adjustments, if any, would you like to make to the Session 1 chart (pages 22–23) that would help other members of the group know how to companion you well?

- Looking ahead, what would you like to be different about your participation or the way you relate to other members of the group? What hopes do you have for these relationships over the next three sessions?

**Individual Activity:** **What I Want to Remember** (2 minutes)

Complete this activity on your own.

1. Briefly review the outline and any notes you took.
2. In the space below, write down the most significant thing you gained in this session—from the teaching, activities, or discussions.

*What I want to remember from this session ...*

## Closing Prayer

Close your time together with prayer.

## SESSION 3 PERSONAL STUDY

### Read and Learn

Read chapters 9–12 of *Beyond Boundaries*. Use the space below to note any insights or questions you want to bring to the next group session.

### Study and Reflect

1. An essential step in being ready to move beyond boundaries is learning to increasingly trust your defining boundaries—the values and characteristics that make you "you."[5] One way to intentionally stretch yourself and develop more trust in your defining boundaries is to normalize telling the truth in your relationships. That means routinely sharing your opinions, feelings, thoughts, and values with the other people in your life. How would you assess your overall comfort level with sharing yourself in this way? Check the box next to the statement (list of options continues on next page) that best describes your response.

   ☐ The truth? I can't handle the truth!
   ☐ The truth is … Oh, look, a bird!
   ☐ I love that whole truthiness vibe.

---

5. For a quick review and examples of defining boundaries, see "Two Kinds of Boundaries" on pages 26–28.

☐ Naked truth has its place, but I feel just a tad bit more comfortable in a loincloth, don't you?

☐ I am all about the truth, the whole truth, and nothing but the truth.

☐ Other:

What kinds of people or circumstances tend to make it more difficult for you to routinely share your opinions, feelings, thoughts, and values?

What connections do you make between these kinds of difficult people or circumstances and the rules—spoken or unspoken—about what you could and could not say out loud when you were growing up? Were you generally encouraged to say what you thought, or pretty much expected to keep your opinions to yourself?

In what ways, if any, has a failure to share your thoughts and feelings contributed to your relational difficulties?

2. Learning to trust your defining boundaries by normalizing truth-telling doesn't mean life becomes an endless series of big-deal conversations, dramatic confrontations,

71

or heart-to-heart talks. As necessary as such interactions sometimes are, most of the time it just means being willing to share the simple truth about what you think or feel in the moment. To get a clearer picture of what this might look like in everyday life, read the personal story John Townsend shares in "A Defining Connection with Truth" on pages 72–73. Then respond to the questions below.

In what ways do you relate or not relate to John's friend in the story?

What concerns you and what excites you about more routinely sharing your opinions, feelings, thoughts, and values with the other people in your life?

## A DEFINING CONNECTION WITH TRUTH

I have a friend who doesn't define himself well. He checks out the relational climate—other people's opinions—before venturing his own opinion. One night we were planning to go to dinner, and I asked him what kind of food he wanted. "Well, what do you like?" he asked. Normally, that kind of question is okay with me, but this wasn't the first time he'd worked the conversation this way, so I decided to push the envelope a little.

"I always go first here," I said. "C'mon, what do you really want?"

"I don't care, whatever you want," he said.

"Are you sure about that?"

"Sure, I'm sure."

"I was thinking that a fast-food drive-through dinner sounds good."

Nothing wrong with that, but I was not in the mood for it and figured neither was he. He laughed and said, "Oh yeah, sure," as if I were joking. I was serious and started driving to a fast-food place.

"Are you kidding?" he asked, looking incredulous.

"No," I said, "if you don't have an opinion, that's where we're going."

"Actually, I feel like Chinese tonight."

"Glad to hear it," I said, and turned the car around. Then I made sure he knew I thought it was great that he put out an opinion.

Now that's a lighthearted story, but it makes a point. Perhaps you're not as afraid as my friend is to define yourself, but you may be close. Instead of waiting to see if the coast is clear, get in the habit of saying what you observe, think, like, or don't like. People may agree or not agree. You may end up with fast food for dinner. But as you normalize truth telling in your relationships, you will find it easier to trust that your defining boundaries are good and that they will help you connect to others in healthy ways.

*Beyond Boundaries*, pages 120–121

3. Every relationship is impacted by the accumulation of "reveal" or "conceal" decisions both people make. Some of these decisions are small and some not so small. The

bigger the potential reveal, the bigger the relational risk. Note how this dynamic plays out in a story from the gospel of Mark.

> A large crowd followed and pressed around him. And a woman was there who had been subject to bleeding for twelve years. She had suffered a great deal under the care of many doctors and had spent all she had, yet instead of getting better she grew worse. When she heard about Jesus, she came up behind him in the crowd and touched his cloak, because she thought, "If I just touch his clothes, I will be healed." Immediately her bleeding stopped and she felt in her body that she was freed from her suffering.
>
> At once Jesus realized that power had gone out from him. He turned around in the crowd and asked, "Who touched my clothes?"
>
> "You see the people crowding against you," his disciples answered, "and yet you can ask, 'Who touched me?'"
>
> But Jesus kept looking around to see who had done it. Then the woman, knowing what had happened to her, came and fell at his feet and, trembling with fear, told him the whole truth. He said to her, "Daughter, your faith has healed you. Go in peace and be freed from your suffering." *Mark 5:24b–34*

The illness from which the woman suffered was not merely physical, it was intensely relational. As a result of her constant uterine bleeding, she would have been considered ceremonially unclean and shunned by her community—for twelve years. Though desperate for healing, she did not want to risk more shame and rejection—from Jesus or the crowd—by revealing herself or her illness in public.

How do you recognize yourself in this woman's suffering and her conflicting desires—to be healed and connected, yet also to remain hidden?

Knowing that her physical suffering was already healed, why do you think Jesus insists that she reveal herself?

Although the woman is instantly healed of her bleeding while still hidden, she receives something more from Jesus when she overcomes her fears and tells the "whole truth" about herself. How would you describe what she would have missed out on if she had refused to reveal herself?

What might you be missing out on when you choose to conceal parts of yourself in your relationships?

If you could overcome your fears, how do you hope sharing the "whole truth" about who you are might change you—and your relationships?

4. In addition to normalizing truthfulness, another essential step in being ready to move beyond boundaries is learning to let your values transform your desires. This is a little like what happens in the physical world when you get serious about working out and eating right. If you do it long enough, high-fat or sugary junk food just isn't as appealing as something healthier. Your investment in healthy values and behaviors changes what you are drawn to. In the relational realm, the healthier your values become, the more you will find yourself drawn to healthier people. That's how, over time, your values transform your desires.

To understand more about the connection between values and desires, read "Three Core Values That Transform Desires" on page 78. Then respond to the following questions.

Reflect on some of the patterns you recognize in your difficult relationships. What unhealthy dynamics tend to characterize the kind of people you find yourself drawn to? Write two or three dynamics in the left column on the chart (page 77). Then use the right column to identify a value that could transform what you're drawn to. It might be one of the three core values you just read about or your own value.

| UNHEALTHY DYNAMICS THAT CHARACTERIZE MY DIFFICULT RELATIONSHIPS | VALUES THAT COULD TRANSFORM WHAT I AM DRAWN TO IN RELATIONSHIPS |
|---|---|
| I tend to be drawn to people who avoid talking about problems or anything unpleasant. | Transparency—I will not hide parts of myself or avoid talking about problems. |
| I like to be around people who seem to be successful and have it all together. I tend to gloss over their character flaws—which almost always turn out to be major. | Honesty—I will not distort reality by diminishing or overlooking character flaws. |
|  |  |
|  |  |
|  |  |

Values must be something you think about all through your life, that you talk about with people, and that dictate your behaviors and attitudes. In what ways do you sense God may be inviting you to take a next step with the values you identified on the chart?

## THREE CORE VALUES
## THAT TRANSFORM DESIRES

*The value of following God.* God is the center of the universe and of your life. As Rick Warren says, "It's not about you." It's about God. Seek his ways and his guidance. The healthiest life is also the holiest life, because holiness is living a life set apart (that is, clearly defined) for God's use.

*The value of vulnerable relationships.* If relationship is one of God's primary delivery systems for providing what we need, it makes sense that relationship should be a high value for you. There are few experiences more positive and rewarding than knowing someone and being known at a deep level. Once you have this experience, it's easy to get used to it and ultimately to require it for yourself.

*The value of honesty.* Dare to be honest. Tell the truth. It is a value for you, but one that needs to be exercised in your life. Using it prevents you from trying to adjust reality in order to fit a bad situation. Once the truth is out, either you will help the other person change or you will face the matter squarely and adapt in a healthier way. And you will find that you are more attracted to people of the truth, the way you have become a person of the truth.

*Beyond Boundaries*, pages 132–138

## Guided Prayer

*God, thank you for using my relationships to teach me more about you and more about myself.*

*I want all of my relationships to be characterized by truth, but I also have some fears about doing that. I am afraid that ...*

*I also want my values to transform my desires. Please help me to live out my values, especially the value of ... I need your help because ...*

*The main thing that stands out to me from this study is ... I especially need your guidance with this because ...*

*Thank you, Lord, for being a Savior who knows the truth about me and loves me still. Amen.*

# Knowing When the Other Person Is Ready
## ASKING THE RIGHT QUESTIONS

The desire for transformation lies deep in every human heart. This is why people enter therapy, join health clubs, get into recovery groups, read self-help books, attend motivational seminars, and make New Year's resolutions. The possibility of transformation is the essence of hope. Psychologist Aaron Beck says that the single belief most toxic to a relationship is the belief that the other person cannot change.

John Ortberg, *The Life You've Always Wanted*

## Group Discussion: Checking In (5 minutes)

Welcome to Session 4 of *Beyond Boundaries*. A key part of getting to know God better is sharing your journey with others. Before watching the video, briefly check in with each other about your experience since the last session. For example:

- How did the last session impact you, your relationships with others, or your relationship with God?
- What insights did you discover in the personal study or in the chapters you read from the *Beyond Boundaries* book?
- What questions would you like to ask the other members of your group?

## Video: Knowing When the Other Person Is Ready (17 minutes)

Play the video segment for Session 4. As you watch, use the accompanying outline (pages 82–84) to follow along or to take notes on anything that stands out to you.

### Notes

This session is about assessing the characteristics and behavior of another person so you can know if they're ready to move beyond boundaries too.

Never let charm trump character; always let character trump charm.

## KNOWING WHEN THE OTHER PERSON IS READY

Five questions to assess the other person's readiness:

1. Does this person care about his or her impact on you?

   "Encourage one another daily, as long as it is called 'Today,' so that none of you may be hardened by sin's deceitfulness" (Hebrews 3:13).

   Is this person willing to see how they can discourage, scare, and frustrate you? Or how they can bring you joy and help you feel peaceful and loved?

2. Is this person (really) connected to good people?

   "[Serve] one another as good stewards of the manifold grace of God" (1 Peter 4:10 NASB).

3. Is the timing righ t? Can this person handle a relationship with you?

   People are in different seasons of life. Not every person is ready for a relationship.

4. For dating and marriage: Does this person go beyond passion?

Look at their language. Can they convey vulnerability as well as romance and passion?

5. Has this person addressed the real problem?

Don't be happy with a do-over. You must go into repentance.

Action steps

1. Check out your two closest friends.

Say to them, "I want to know how I impact you for good or for bad. And I want to tell you how you impact me."

2. Evaluate the person you're considering taking a risk with.

Look at their life and their habits.

This is not about judging someone. It's about steward-ship—of your life, your energy, your heart, and your time.

**Group Discussion** (36 minutes)

Take a few minutes to talk about what you just watched.

1. What part of the teaching had the most impact on you?

2. For the remainder of the discussion, choose a focus person—one relationship you have that will be the focus of your thoughts and comments for this session. Even if it's not your most difficult relationship, choose a relationship you feel comfortable discussing within the group. (If you completed the personal studies for Sessions 1 or 2, you may wish to refer to the list of names you wrote on the chart on page 33 or to the person you identified in question 1 on page 48.) As with all group discussions, confidentiality is essential and nothing that is shared within the group should be discussed outside the group.

   Take a moment to identify your focus person and write that person's name below.

Briefly share with the group the person you chose and why.

## *Does This Person Care about His or Her Impact on You?*

3. God tells us in many ways to be aware of how we respond to each other and to be mindful of the impact we have on one another. Here are two examples of biblical truths and what they reveal about the power we have to impact each other:

   *Biblical truth:* "Therefore confess your sins to each other and pray for each other so that you may be healed" (James 5:16).

   *Relational impact:* God uses us to play a role in healing each other.

   *Biblical truth:* "Above all, love each other deeply, because love covers over a multitude of sins" (1 Peter 4:8).

   *Relational impact:* Our love for each other helps us deal with the sins we commit.

   Go around the group and have a different person read aloud each of the passages on page 87. As the verses are read, underline any words or phrases that stand out to you. (Wait to identify and discuss the relational impacts until after reading through the list.) You may wish to read through the list twice to give everyone time to listen and respond.

86

*Biblical truth:* "Therefore let us stop passing judgment on one another. Instead, make up your mind not to put any stumbling block or obstacle in the way of a brother or sister" (Romans 14:13).

*Relational impact:*

*Biblical truth:* "Let us therefore make every effort to do what leads to peace and to mutual edification" (Romans 14:19).

*Relational impact:*

*Biblical truth:* "Accept one another, then, just as Christ accepted you, in order to bring praise to God" (Romans 15:7).

*Relational impact:*

*Biblical truth:* "You, my brothers and sisters, were called to be free. But do not use your freedom to indulge the flesh; rather, serve one another humbly in love. For the entire law is fulfilled in keeping this one command: 'Love your neighbor as yourself.' If you bite and devour each other, watch out or you will be destroyed by each other" (Galatians 5:13–15).

*Relational impact:*

- What do these biblical truths reveal about the relational impact we have on one another?

- Which truth resonates most with you? Why?

4. To what degree has a lack of awareness about the impact you have on each other been a factor in the relationship with your focus person?

## Is This Person (Really) Connected to Good People?

5. Pair up with one other person for this discussion question.

Listed on pages 89–90 are five indications that someone is genuinely connected to good people. Taking turns back and forth with your partner, read through the list out loud. Then go back through each statement one at a time. If you find it helpful, use the numbered continuums to assess the relationship with your focus person. Briefly share with your partner you and your focus person's status for each characteristic.

*You share similar healthy values with these people.* You and the good people your focus person is connected to both value such things as God, relationship, honesty, responsibility, and authenticity.

| 1 | 2 | 3 | 4 | 5 |
|---|---|---|---|---|
| Completely untrue | Mostly untrue | Somewhat true | Mostly true | Completely true |

*You like these people.* You don't have to force yourself to enjoy being with the people your focus person is connected to.

| 1 | 2 | 3 | 4 | 5 |
|---|---|---|---|---|
| Completely untrue | Mostly untrue | Somewhat true | Mostly true | Completely true |

*You see vulnerability in the relationship.* Your focus person not only hangs out with these good people but also gets real with them.

| 1 | 2 | 3 | 4 | 5 |
|---|---|---|---|---|
| Completely untrue | Mostly untrue | Somewhat true | Mostly true | Completely true |

*Your person relates to good people outside of you.* Your focus person spends time with good people because it is important to him/her, not just because your focus person thinks it will please you.

| 1 | 2 | 3 | 4 | 5 |
|---|---|---|---|---|
| Completely untrue | Mostly untrue | Somewhat true | Mostly true | Completely true |

*You see good fruit in the person.* Your focus person is becoming a better person — not staying the same or getting worse — through relationships with good people.

| 1 | 2 | 3 | 4 | 5 |
|---|---|---|---|---|
| Completely untrue | Mostly untrue | Somewhat true | Mostly true | Completely true |

Based on your assessment and discussion of the five indications, would you say that your focus person is or is not connected to good people?

## Can This Person Handle a Relationship with You Right Now?

6. How would you describe the kind of relational care or help you want when you are struggling in some way — whether it's feeling discouraged, empty, fatigued, stressed, lonely, angry, frustrated, or prickly? For example, do you need a listening ear, a hug, quiet time together, an expression of interest you don't have to ask for, encouragement, etc.?

7. Based on what you know about your focus person's season of life and any challenges he/she may have, do you feel like your focus person has the emotional and relational capacity to provide the kind of relational care you want at this time?

## For Dating and Marriage: Does This Person Go Beyond Passion?

8. In a dating or marriage relationship, one way to assess whether or not the other person is ready to move beyond boundaries is to focus on their language. Are they capable of expressing vulnerability as well as passion? Briefly review the examples of both kinds of language below, and then answer the related questions on page 92.

| Romantic Language | Vulnerable Language |
|---|---|
| *You are so amazing.* | *How are you?* |
| *You are incredibly attractive.* | *Tell me more about that.* |
| *I've never met anyone like you.* | *How did the boss make you feel when he said that?* |
| *I want you so much.* | *Did I hurt your feelings when I did that?* |
| *I've never felt like this with anyone (on the first date!).* | *How are you and I doing?* |
| *I feel like I've known you all my life (also on the first date!).* | *I'd like to tell you more about me and know more about you at a deeper level.* |
| *I could be like this with you forever.* | *I feel like I can be myself with you.* |
| *You're all I think about.* | *I've struggled as well.* |

- How would you characterize the difference between the two kinds of language?

- If your focus person is a spouse or someone you're dating, how would you describe his/her capacity for vulnerable communication?

## *Is the Big Problem Being Solved the Right Way?*

9. In a relationship where there has been a problem, it's important to discern whether or not the other person has addressed the real problem and changed as a result. Evidence of authentic transformation includes four components:

   *Confession:* A confession includes both the other person's admission of the truth about what they have done and their acknowledgment that the behavior impacted you.

   *Ownership:* To own a behavior is to take responsibility for it, without blame or excuse.

   *Remorse:* Remorse is an expression of deep regret by the other person for what they have done to you. Authentic remorse focuses on conveying comfort and empathy for you rather than focusing on their guilt.

   *Changed behavior:* Authentic confession, ownership, and remorse should naturally lead to changed behavior. However, it's important to remember that what you're really looking for is not merely improvement in the other person's behavior but transformation of who they are as a person.

- Transformation that leads to the restoration of relationships is a foundational biblical value (Matthew 6:12–15; Luke 17:3–4; Galatians 6:1; Ephesians 4:31–32; Colossians 3:12–13). Within your church or larger Christian community, how have you experienced this process personally or witnessed others working through it? (NOTE: It's not necessary to share all the details and it's wise to protect confidentiality. Focus your comments on how the parties were impacted individually, what happened in their relationship, and any insights you may have gained.)

- How do you hope the restoration process with your focus person might be similar to or different from what you've previously experienced or witnessed others working through?

10. Take a moment to touch base with each other about how you're doing in the group. Use one of the sentence starters below, or your own statement, to help the group learn more about the best way to companion you.

   *I want to give you permission to challenge me more about ...*

   *An area where I really need your help or sensitivity is ...*

   *It always helps me to feel more connected to the group when ...*

   *Something I've learned about myself because of this group is ...*

**Individual Activity: What I Want to Remember** (2 minutes)

Complete this activity on your own.

1. Briefly review the outline and any notes you took.
2. In the space below, write down the most significant thing you gained in this session—from the teaching, activities, or discussions.

   *What I want to remember from this session ...*

## Closing Prayer

Close your time together with prayer.

## SESSION 4 PERSONAL STUDY

### Read and Learn

Read chapters 13–17 of *Beyond Boundaries*. Use the space below to note any insights or questions you want to bring to the next group session.

### Study and Reflect

1. Choose a focus person for this personal study, ideally someone with whom you have or once had a protective boundary. You may wish to refer to the list of names you wrote on the chart on page 33 or to the person(s) you identified in question 1 on page 48 or question 2 on page 85. Write that person's name below.

2. On the video, John presented five questions you can use to assess the other person's readiness to move beyond boundaries. Review the brief descriptions for the five questions (pages 96–98) and circle the number on each continuum that best describes where you think your focus person is at with that part of the process.

   Then, in the space provided following each continuum, briefly note the evidence you have for your assessment. Evidence is proof—something concrete—that demonstrates whether or not the other person is experiencing authentic life change. If your focus person hasn't yet begun this process, describe instead the kind of evidence you hope for. For example, what evidence would demonstrate to you that your focus person cares about his/her impact on you or is really connected to good people?

*Does this person care about his/her impact on you?* When people care about the impact they have on others, it doesn't mean that they never make mistakes. It means that when someone they hurt brings it to their attention, they are more concerned about the well-being of the person they hurt than they are about their own comfort or desire to defend themselves.

| 1 | 2 | 3 | 4 | 5 | 6 | 7 | 8 | 9 | 10 |
|---|---|---|---|---|---|---|---|---|---|
| I have no evidence that my focus person cares about his/her impact on me. | | | | I have some evidence that my focus person cares about his/her impact on me. | | | | I have significant evidence that my focus person cares about his/her impact on me. | |

Evidence I have (or hope for):

*Is this person (really) connected to good people?* Being really connected to good people is about more than hanging out with friends. Among other things, it requires shared values, vulnerability, and becoming a better, healthier person because of the relationships with these good people.

| 1 | 2 | 3 | 4 | 5 | 6 | 7 | 8 | 9 | 10 |
|---|---|---|---|---|---|---|---|---|---|
| I have no evidence that my focus person is really connected to good people. | | | | I have some evidence that my focus person is really connected to good people. | | | | I have significant evidence that my focus person is really connected to good people. | |

96

Evidence I have (or hope for):

*Can this person handle a relationship with you right now?* Being able to engage in relationship requires a capacity to provide care and attention to the other person. When facing a difficult season of life or other personal challenges, a person may or may not have this capacity.

**1    2    3    4    5    6    7    8    9    10**

I have no evidence that my focus person is able to handle a relationship with me right now.

I have some evidence that my focus person is able to handle a relationship with me right now.

I have significant evidence that my focus person is able to handle a relationship with me right now.

Evidence I have (or hope for):

*For dating and marriage: Does this person go beyond passion?* Passion has its place, but passion alone will not sustain or deepen a relationship. Both people need to be interested in the inner life of the other person and to make vulnerable communication a routine part of the relationship.

**1    2    3    4    5    6    7    8    9    10**

I have no evidence that my focus person is ready to go beyond passion and to be vulnerable.

I have some evidence that my focus person is ready to go beyond passion and to be vulnerable.

I have significant evidence that my focus person is ready to go beyond passion and to be vulnerable.

97

Evidence I have (or hope for):

*Is the problem being solved the right way?* The person with the problem that was previously an obstacle in the relationship must be in the process of transformation. Evidence of authentic heart change includes confession, ownership, remorse, and changed behavior.

| 1 | 2 | 3 | 4 | 5 | 6 | 7 | 8 | 9 | 10 |
|---|---|---|---|---|---|---|---|---|----|
| I have no evidence that my focus person's problem is being solved the right way. | | | | I have some evidence that my focus person's problem is being solved the right way. | | | | I have significant evidence that my focus person's problem is being solved the right way. | |

Evidence I have (or hope for):

3. In the process of working through the five questions to assess the readiness of your focus person, which question(s), if any, struck a chord in you about yourself? For example, perhaps another relationship came to mind and you thought, *I've failed to care about my impact on this person*, or *There is a problem in this relationship I need to confess and own.* Write down the question and briefly describe why it struck a chord in you.

How does reflecting on your own relational challenges influence the way you view or feel about your focus person?

4. One way people in a relationship demonstrate that they care about the impact they have on each other is in how they communicate when a problem arises. Are their responses to each other caring or uncaring? To get a clearer picture of what this looks like in everyday life, read "Caring and Uncaring Responses" on pages 100–101. Then respond to the questions below.

What stands out most to you about the differences between the caring and the uncaring responses?

How do you tend to respond when you get an uncaring response or when someone doesn't appear to care about the impact they have on you? For example, do you respond in kind? Try to protect yourself as best you can? Just take it and hope things will get better?

## CARING AND UNCARING RESPONSES

You need to be a person who cares about how you affect others and require that of those who matter to you.... Here are some examples of caring and uncaring responses people have in various situations.

*Situation*: A husband is overspending and his wife mentions the problem to him.

*Uncaring response*: I have a right to the money as much as you do. I can choose, and you need to trust me.

*Caring response*: I didn't know how much the spending scared you. Let's look at the budget and figure something out.

*Situation*: An adult child is living with his parents and it's time to get a job and move out.

*Uncaring response*: Get off my back! You guys are so unsupportive.

*Caring response*: I appreciate the break you're giving me. Let's come up with a launch plan that works.

*Situation*: A wife is chronically late and the husband has brought it up.

*Uncaring response*: You're always micromanaging me.

*Caring response*: I guess it's hard when I tell you I'll be home at 6:00 for dinner and it's always 6:45.

*Situation*: A direct report is not attuned to the culture of his organization and the team is suffering because of it.

*Uncaring response*: I'm doing my best. You don't see the things I do for this company.

*Caring response*: Tell me what I'm doing. I want to fix this.

*Situation*: A husband has a critical mom and his wife is getting the brunt of it.

*Uncaring response*: Just be nice to my mom and stop griping.

*Caring response*: I'm sorry for not standing up to my mom when she criticizes you.

*Situation*: A friend takes a long time to repay a loan.

*Uncaring response*: I don't think you realize all the things I do for you.

*Caring response*: I'm really sorry I haven't kept up to date on this with you. How soon do you need it?

*Situation*: A husband's drinking is concerning his wife.

*Uncaring response*: If you wouldn't disrespect me, I wouldn't have to drink; it's my way of coping with you.

*Caring response*: I'm so sorry I scare you when I drink. I'll never drink like that again, and if I do, tell me, and I'll get help.

Don't give up hope if you are getting uncaring responses. It may not be a sign to find the exit door. The person you're interested in connecting with might just need a little coaching. Then they understand that it's important to you to know how they affect you. But don't take any more steps toward vulnerability until you talk about this. If it's a little defensiveness or cluelessness and the lights come on when you talk about it, and their behavior begins to change, then they pass that test and it's safe to proceed.

*Beyond Boundaries*, pages 161–162

5. Desiring and, ultimately, requiring that someone be concerned about his or her impact on you is not a sign of self-absorption but a sign of health. It is your responsibility and evidence of self-stewardship. You only have one heart. If you repeatedly subject it to bad treatment or constantly have to protect yourself, you are not taking good care of that heart. The Bible makes it clear how important this is:

> Above all else, guard your heart, for everything you do
> flows from it.                                      *Proverbs 4:23*

And it's encouraging to know that none of us are alone in our heart-guarding work:

> [God's] peace will guard your hearts and minds as you
> live in Christ Jesus.                       *Philippians 4:7b NLT*

When you consider the relationship with your focus person, how might you need to guard your heart right now?

With your focus person, or in any of your relationships, how do you need to experience God's peace to guard your heart and your mind?

## Guided Prayer

*God, thank you for giving me a wise path to follow as I take steps to develop trusting relationships.*

*I know it's possible to assess how ready—and trustworthy—the other people in my life are, but it still isn't easy. Please give me your eyes so I can see my relationships the way you do. I especially need your help with ...*

*I ask for your strength and your guidance as I learn how to guard my heart from ...*

*I also want your peace to guard my heart and my mind. Sometimes it seems like my anxious thoughts about my relationships are even more difficult to deal with than the relationships themselves. I especially need your peace regarding ...*

*Lord, in all things, at all times, you are always trustworthy. I surrender myself to your care, your guidance, and your love. Amen.*

# Moving into Relationship, Part 1
## UNDERSTANDING THE DANCE, PREPARING FOR THE TALK

Belief and trust are essential to intimacy and self-disclosure. The more we feel trusted and believed in, the more we are willing to reveal and the more we understand each other.

Bill Donahue, *In the Company of Jesus*

## Group Discussion: Checking In (5 minutes)

Welcome to Session 5 of *Beyond Boundaries*. A key part of getting to know God better is sharing your journey with others. Before watching the video, briefly check in with each other about your experience since the last session. For example:

- How did the last session impact you, your relationships with others, or your relationship with God?
- What insights did you discover in the personal study or in the chapters you read from the *Beyond Boundaries* book?
- What questions would you like to ask the other members of your group?

## Video: Moving into Relationship Part 1 (16 minutes)

Play the video segment for Session 5. As you watch, use the accompanying outline (pages 106–108) to follow along or to take notes on anything that stands out to you.

### Notes

Every good and life-giving relationship should be two people who are connected but separate.

You have a relational pattern—a set of identifiable behaviors that may or may not work for you. This is your relational dance.

Three elements of the relational dance: connection, responsibility, and freedom

1. Connection

How vulnerable are the people in the relationship and how much initiative do they take to make the connection?

"Jesus replied: 'Love the Lord your God with all your heart and with all your soul and with all your mind.' This is the first and greatest commandment. And the second is like it: 'Love your neighbor as yourself'" (Matthew 22:37–39).

2. Responsibility

Relationships may be about love, but they're also about ownership—about me taking responsibility for my part and how I affect the other person.

"For each one should carry their own load" (Galatians 6:5).

3. Freedom

Every good relationship gives up control of the relationship and allows freedom.

"It is for freedom that Christ has set us free. Stand firm, then, and do not let yourselves be burdened again by a yoke of slavery" (Galatians 5:1).

Learning how to have "the talk"

"But everything exposed by the light becomes visible—and everything that is illuminated becomes a light" (Ephesians 5:13).

1. State what you value and desire.

This is a really important relationship to me.

2. State your concern.

There is something that I'm finding a problem.

3. Establish ground rules.

Ground rules are a suggestion you have that's specific to help things get better.

4. Ask for buy-in.

Buy-in identifies the benefit. It means: if this happens, our relationship gets better.

Action steps

1. Identify which of the three elements you need to work on in your own relational dance.

2. Have a practice talk.

## Talking the Talk

Having "the talk" is an essential and significant step for moving beyond boundaries and into relationship. It can also be a little intimidating or anxiety-producing if you aren't sure what to say or try to wing it without any preparation. Even though it might seem awkward at first, practicing the talk with someone else ahead of time is the best way to be prepared for the actual talk you need to have in any relationship. So this session is a little different from previous sessions. It's designed to help you identify and organize what you want to say, and then to practice actually saying it—all in a safe setting where it's okay to make some mistakes and try again.

For the purpose of this session, assume that you and the person with whom you want to have a relationship have both worked through the process and are ready to move beyond boundaries. Even if the relationship you're considering isn't yet in a place to have this conversation, practicing the talk is still a valuable way to prepare yourself for it—and to give your relational muscles a strength-building workout. Practice doesn't make perfect, but it will make having the real talk a whole lot easier.

NOTE: In order to complete the session in one hour, it's important to adhere to the suggested times for all activities and discussions. Before beginning the Individual Activity, appoint one person to be a timekeeper. The Individual Activity is 12 minutes. To make sure everyone is on track throughout the activity, the timekeeper should alert the group twice—at the halfway point (after 6 minutes) and when just 1 minute remains. If you have more than one hour for your meeting, you may wish to allow additional time for everyone to work through the Individual Activity.

**Individual Activity:** **Preparing for the Talk** (12 minutes)

Complete this activity on your own.

1. Identify a focus person for this activity. Choose a relationship in which there has been a problem you want to talk about. Write that person's name below.

Briefly describe the problem you need to talk about with this person.

2. With your focus person in mind and using the provided examples as a reference, work through the four components of the talk presented on pages 111–114. Don't worry about making it perfect or scripting every word. You can work on it more on your own at a later time. For now, use the four prompts to identify the main issues and to organize your thoughts.

110

*(1) State what you value and desire.* A statement of *value* is about where you are now in your feelings for the person; a statement of *desire* is about what you would like to see in the future. With these statements, you acknowledge why the focus person is important to you and share the hopes you have for the relationship. The most effective statements are simple, direct, and vulnerable.

**Examples:**

*Our friendship is really important to me, and I'd like it to be even stronger.*

*I value the contributions you've made to our organization, and I value your friendship as well. I want us to work well together.*

*Even though things have been rough, I am for us. I want to find a healthy way to talk about our differences.*

My value and desire statement:

*(2) State your concern.* Name what happened in the past, acknowledge your part in it, and state what you don't want to happen in the future. Without blaming or being a victim, you briefly state the facts of your relational history, how you understand your own contribution to the difficulties, and how you could be hurt if the problem isn't addressed.

**Examples:**

*Because of my parent's problems when I was a kid, I ended up being the caregiver for my younger brother and sister. I'm still trying to break that pattern in my adult relationships and I don't want it to be a problem for us.*

*We've missed multiple client deadlines because your part of the project wasn't done on time. For my part, I want to acknowledge that I have overloaded you lately with some big assignments. We need to address this so we don't risk losing clients.*

*Part of our relationship has been dealing with your anger issues. Anger scares me so I always try to avoid you when you're angry or avoid talking about something that might make you angry. I don't want to feel like I have to walk on eggshells around you anymore.*

My concern statement:

*(3) Establish ground rules.* Ground rules are suggestions you have that address the concerns you raised. Once agreed upon, they provide a way for both of you to monitor the process of improving the relationship. To be effective, ground rules must be actionable, measurable, and specific. Keep them simple and few.

**Examples:**

*When we get together, would you mind for a while taking the initiative to ask how I'm doing?*

*For the next six weeks, I need you to complete your work on or before the deadlines we've agreed to.*

*When we have a disagreement, I'd like us to sit down and talk about it calmly. Neither of us will leave the room in the middle of it nor raise our voices.*

My suggestion for ground rules:

*(4) Ask for buy-in.* This is where you identify the benefit. In other words: *If this happens, our relationship gets better.* Conclude with a question that asks for buy-in.

**Examples:**

*If we are able to be more mutual in reaching out, I'm going to feel so great about our friendship. Besides that, I want to hear from you about any areas I'm not doing well in so I can work on that too. Are you okay with all this?*

*Meeting or beating your deadlines will communicate to me and to the team that you're serious about improving your performance. I believe you can make a significant contribution here and I want to help you make that happen. Does this sound good to you too?*

*If we can find a healthy way to talk through our disagreements, I will feel so much more secure and connected to you. I really want us to be closer and I know that will require me to make some changes too. How do you feel about moving ahead in this way?*

My request for buy-in:

3. Briefly review your responses to the four prompts. For each one, circle key words or phrases that capture the gist of what you want to say. Write these words and phrases on the chart below so you'll have all your notes in one place.

| FOUR COMPONENTS OF THE TALK | MY TALK: KEY WORDS AND PHRASES |
|---|---|
| 1. State what you value and desire. | |
| 2. State your concern. | |
| 3. Establish ground rules. | |
| 4. Ask for buy-in. | |

NOTE: The timekeeper's job is not done yet! To make sure everyone is on track throughout the Partner Activity, the timekeeper should alert the group after 6 minutes and direct partners to move promptly into the feedback portion of the activity (step 4). This assures that partners will be ready to switch roles within a minute or two and still have enough time for both people to complete the activity. Alert the group again when just 2 minutes remain, encouraging partners to once again move into the feedback portion of the activity (step 4).

## Partner Activity: Practicing the Talk (16 minutes)

1. Pair up with one other person.
2. Decide who will go first.
3. Briefly tell your partner about the problem you want to address with your focus person. Then present your talk as if your partner were your focus person. It's okay to glance at the key words and phrases on your chart (page 115) if you need a prompt. Partners should listen supportively and make mental notes about anything that seems unclear.
4. Once the speaker has given his/her talk, the listener provides feedback about what worked well and what could be clearer.
5. Switch roles—the speaker becomes the listener and the listener becomes the speaker. Repeat steps 1–4.

**Group Discussion:** **Talking about the Talk** (9 minutes)

1. What was it like to practice your talk?

2. How would you describe your comfort level with having the talk with your focus person? Do you feel pretty confident or do you need more practice?

3. Throughout this curriculum, you've had the opportunity to devote a portion of your discussion time to talking about your relationships within the group, and especially about how to companion each other well. What are your observations about this portion of the discussion in every session? For example, what, if any, differences do you notice in yourself and in the group when you're talking about your relationships within the group (rather than about the content of the curriculum or your other relationships)? Do you tend to look forward to this portion of the discussion or secretly hope you'll run out of time before you get to it? Why?

**Individual Activity:** **What I Want to Remember** (2 minutes)

Complete this activity on your own.

1. Briefly review the outline and any notes you took.
2. In the space below, write down the most significant thing you gained in this session — from the teaching, activities, or discussions.

   *What I want to remember from this session ...*

### Closing Prayer

Close your time together with prayer.

## GET A HEAD START ON THE DISCUSSION FOR SESSION 6

As part of the group discussion for Session 6, you'll have an opportunity to talk about what you've learned and experienced together throughout the *Beyond Boundaries* curriculum. Between now and your next meeting, consider taking a few moments to review the previous sessions and identify the teaching, discussions, or activities that stand out most to you. If you'd like, use the worksheet on pages 119–120 to briefly summarize the highlights of what you've learned and experienced.

## SESSION 6 HEAD START WORKSHEET

Take a few moments to reflect on what you've learned and experienced throughout the *Beyond Boundaries* curriculum. You may want to review notes from the video teaching, your comments in the "What I Want to Remember" section at the end of each group session, responses in the personal studies, etc. Here are some questions you might consider as part of your review:

- What struggles or progress did I experience related to this session?
- What was the most important thing I learned about myself or my relationships in this session?
- How did I experience God's presence or leading related to this session?
- What are my highlights from the group or personal studies for this session?
- How did this session impact my relationships with the other people in the group?

Use the spaces provided below and on page 120 to briefly summarize what you've learned and experienced for each session.

### Session 1
Understanding the Problem: Reclaiming Trust (pages 13–36)

## Session 2

Knowing When You're Ready, Part 1: Unlearning Old Ways
(pages 37–58)

## Session 3

Knowing When You're Ready, Part 2: Learning New Ways
(pages 59–79)

## Session 4

Knowing When the Other Person Is Ready: Asking the Right
Questions (pages 81–103)

## Session 5

Moving into Relationship, Part 1: Understanding the Dance,
Preparing for the Talk (pages 105–132)

## SESSION 5 PERSONAL STUDY

### Read and Learn

Read chapter 18 of *Beyond Boundaries*. Use the space below to note any insights or questions you want to bring to the next group session.

### Study and Reflect

In your most significant relationships, you have a pattern or a dance. This dance is made up of identifiable behaviors that cause your relationships to struggle or to thrive. Identifying your dance—the patterned ways you relate to others—and understanding how it impacts your relationships is an essential step for moving beyond boundaries. Three dance steps play an important role in the degree to which your relationships struggle or thrive: *connection, responsibility,* and *freedom.*

1. *Connection.* Connection is about how vulnerable two people are with each other and how much initiative they take in the relationship. You make a connection when you extend yourself in an authentic and vulnerable way to someone else. Of the three dance steps, this is perhaps the most important because the essence of any good relationship is how much two people care about each other. In the best relationships—the ones with a good dance—both people share equally in taking initiative and being vulnerable.

Listed below are five word pairings that contrast vulnerability with invulnerability. Choose a focus person—ideally someone with whom you have or once had a protective boundary. Write that person's name in the space provided. Then assess the current level of vulnerability or invulnerability for both of you. Place an X on each continuum to assess yourself and a dot or circle to assess your focus person (each continuum should have both an X and a dot).

*My focus person*:

VULNERABLE — INVULNERABLE
Exposed — Hidden

VULNERABLE — INVULNERABLE
Capable of being hurt — Defended

VULNERABLE — INVULNERABLE
Sensitive — Uncaring

VULNERABLE — INVULNERABLE
Open — Closed

VULNERABLE — INVULNERABLE
Undefended — Guarded

What vulnerability similarities and differences exist between you and your focus person?

In addition to your focus person, identify two other significant relationships and list all three names below. For each one, assess the balance of initiative between you. For example, is it shared equally at 50/50? Is it imbalanced at 80/20, with you taking initiative 80 percent of the time? Or is it somewhere in between?

**Example**

The initiative balance between me and

_____*Celeste*_____ is ____*40/60*____.

The initiative balance between me and

_____ is _____.

The initiative balance between me and

_____ is _____.

The initiative balance between me and

_____ is _____.

How is your part of the initiative balance the same or different in each relationship? How do you account for the similarities and differences?

The foundation of the Christian faith is love—God's love for us, our love for God and others (Matthew 22:36–39). We know this. And yet we also struggle with it in virtually all our relationships. *What does it really mean to love this person in this moment?* In his letter to the church at Colossae, the apostle Paul provides a brief and instructive description of love in action. As you read through the passage, underline any words or phrases that stand out to you.

> Therefore, as God's chosen people, holy and dearly loved, clothe yourselves with compassion, kindness, humility, gentleness and patience. Bear with each other and forgive one another if any of you has a grievance against someone. Forgive as the Lord forgave you. And over all these virtues put on love, which binds them all together in perfect unity. *Colossians 3:12–14*

For a fresh take on this familiar passage, read it again from *The Message*:

> So, chosen by God for this new life of love, dress in the wardrobe God picked out for you: compassion, kindness, humility, quiet strength, discipline. Be even-tempered, content with second place, quick to forgive an offense. Forgive as quickly and completely as the Master forgave you. And regardless of what else you put on, wear love. It's your basic, all-purpose garment. Never be without it. *Colossians 3:12–14 MSG*

Choose up to five of the phrases you underlined and write them in the left column of the chart on page 125. In the right column, reflect on any connections you make between your words and phrases and the relationship with your focus person. These could include a specific action you feel God may be asking you to take, something you realize is missing (or present) in the relationship, a confession, or anything else that comes to mind when you think about your focus person and that word/phrase.

| WORDS OR PHRASES THAT STAND OUT TO ME | HOW THIS CONNECTS TO THE RELATIONSHIP WITH MY FOCUS PERSON |
|---|---|
| Kindness | Our relationship is struggling, but I can still be kind. |
| Holy and dearly loved | We are both dearly loved by God. |
| Quick to forgive | I struggle with this one. I know I am not quick to forgive in our relationship. |
| | |
| | |
| | |
| | |
| | |

Based on the assessments of vulnerability and initiative, the Colossians passage, and your own experiences and insights, how would you describe the current (or past) connection pattern between you and your focus person?

2. *Responsibility.* Relationships may be about affinity and love, but they're also about ownership. In this relational dance step, each person takes responsibility for their part and how they affect the other person. The apostle Paul puts it this way, "Each one should carry their own load" (Galatians 6:5). Responsibility also includes dependability. Do both people do what they say they will do? Can they be relied on? To get an idea of what responsibility looks like in a relationship, read "The Responsibility Dance" on pages 128–129. Then respond to the questions below.

Use the image of a seesaw balance to do a brief assessment of the responsibility balance in the relationship with your focus person. On page 127 the example on the left shows an even balance, indicating both people take full and equal responsibility for how they impact each other in the relationship. The example on the right shows an uneven balance, indicating that one person takes full responsibility and the other person does not. Draw your own seesaw balance to indicate the degree to which you and your focus person "carry your own load" by taking responsibility for how you impact each other in the relationship.

## Examples

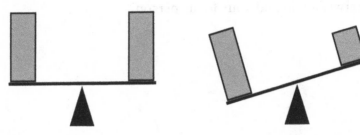

## The Balance of Responsibility in My Relationship

Carrying your own load in a relationship also includes being dependable and doing what you say you will do. Place an X on the two continuums below to assess the degree to which you and your focus person are (or were) dependable within the relationship.

●━━━━━━━━━━━━━━━━━━━━━━━●

I am never dependable.
My focus person is not able
to rely on me.

I am always dependable.
My focus person is
able to rely on me.

●━━━━━━━━━━━━━━━━━━━━━━━●

My focus person is never
dependable. I am not able
to rely on him/her.

My focus person is
always dependable. I am
able to rely on him/her.

Based on the seesaw balance and continuum assessments, and your own insight and experiences, how would you describe the current (or past) responsibility pattern between you and your focus person?

## THE RESPONSIBILITY DANCE

I [John] was working with a couple where the responsibility part of the relational dance was definitely one-sided. The husband, Richard, was the "bad guy"—the one who always seemed to be messing up. When he and his wife, Ellen, were out with friends, Ellen inevitably found a way to make Richard the brunt of all the jokes. She'd point out how he messed up the finances or the vacation plans. She'd describe how disorganized and absentminded he was and how he needed a GPS device because he was always getting lost.

I was at a party once where Ellen kept telling "stupid Richard" stories. Several of us felt a little uncomfortable because Richard was sitting there being the dunce while Ellen went on and on about what a goofball he was. And I could tell that it really hurt Richard. Ellen was a nice person, but she was also one of those people who have to feel superior, like she's got it together all the time. To preserve the relationship, Richard went along and didn't seem to mind being the clown, at least initially. But after a while, it became a problem and he finally had to say, "Could you at least affirm me sometimes? And also acknowledge that you make mistakes too, because it really doesn't feel equal to me."

Before Richard confronted her, Ellen was having fun telling stories at his expense, but she never considered how her comments might be impacting him. In addition, she failed to be dependable with her words. Because Richard never knew how she would treat him—positively or negatively—he felt wary and insecure with her in social settings.

Fortunately, when Richard raised the issue, Ellen got it. She owned her mistakes, took responsibility for the way her words impacted him, and changed her behavior. That's what it means to take responsibility in the relational dance—you own the impact you have on the other person.

*Beyond Boundaries* video

3. *Freedom.* Freedom means both people allow each other to have their own opinions, choices, and values. Things go wrong when one person's views or preferences dominate the relationship. In some cases, the non-dominant person might even feel bad or guilty about disagreeing or making an independent choice, especially if it threatens the relationship. That's a problem. You need to insist on freedom—for yourself and for the other person. Every really good relationship encourages and protects the freedom of both people.

How much freedom do you feel (or did you once feel) in the relationship with your focus person? Circle the number on the continuum below that best describes your response.

| 1 | 2 | 3 | 4 | 5 | 6 | 7 | 8 | 9 | 10 |
|---|---|---|---|---|---|---|---|---|---|
| **No freedom** I always feel significant pressure to change or hide my opinions, choices, and values. | | | | **Moderate freedom** I occasionally feel some pressure to change or hide my opinions, choices, and values. | | | | **Complete freedom** I never feel pressure to change or hide my opinions, choices, and values. | |

129

How do you imagine your focus person might describe the amount of freedom he/she feels (or once felt) in the relationship with you? Circle the number on the continuum below that best describes your response.

| 1 | 2 | 3 | 4 | 5 | 6 | 7 | 8 | 9 | 10 |
|---|---|---|---|---|---|---|---|---|---|

**No freedom**
My focus person would say, "I always feel significant pressure to change or hide my opinions, choices, and values."

**Moderate freedom**
My focus person would say, "I occasionally feel some pressure to change or hide my opinions, choices, and values."

**Complete freedom**
My focus person would say, "I never feel pressure to change or hide my opinions, choices, and values."

What might be your focus person's response if he/she could see the numbers you circled on both continuums? Do you expect there would be surprise, disagreement, or some other response?

Based on the assessments and your own insight and experiences, how would you describe the current (or past) freedom pattern between you and your focus person?

130

4. When something goes wrong or there is an imbalance in the connection, responsibility, or freedom aspects of a relationship, it's important to talk about those issues so the relationship can get better.

Based on your assessments of the relationship with your focus person in this study, what problems or concerns do you feel you will eventually need to talk about?[6]

---

6. For additional guidance on how to talk about problems in a relationship, refer back to the Individual Activity: Preparing for the Talk (pages 110–115). If you missed the Session 5 group meeting, go ahead and complete the Individual Activity for one of the problems you identify.

## Guided Prayer

*God, thank you that the foundation of my faith is your relentless love for me.*

*I confess I often struggle with my part of the love equation—the "loving others" part. My relationships can be so difficult and I don't always handle myself well. I'm really struggling right now with ...*

*In the relationship with my focus person, I ask that you help me ... and help my focus person ...*

*I know that sooner or later I am going to have to have "talks" so that my relationships can get better. Is it okay to just say it? I don't want to! I feel resistant because ...*

*Still, I believe and trust that there is something better for me—and for all the people in my life—if I can learn to talk about problems with the people I care about. What I especially hope will be better is ...*

*Lord, even though it's so hard, thank you for using all of my relationships—especially the difficult ones—to teach me what it really means to love and be loved. Amen.*

# Moving into Relationship, Part 2
## TAKING THE RISK

When you are faithful to the risk and ambivalence of growth, you are engaging your life. The soul loves risk; it is only through the door of risk that growth can enter.

John O'Donohue, *Anam Cara*

## Group Discussion: Checking In (5 minutes)

Welcome to Session 6 of *Beyond Boundaries*. A key part of getting to know God better is sharing your journey with others. Before watching the video, briefly check in with each other about your experience since the last session. For example:

- How did the last session impact you, your relationships with others, or your relationship with God?
- What insights did you discover in the personal study or in the chapters you read from the *Beyond Boundaries* book?
- What questions would you like to ask the other members of your group?

## Video: Moving into Relationship, Part 2 (17 minutes)

Play the video segment for Session 6. As you watch, use the accompanying outline (pages 134–136) to follow along or to take notes on anything that stands out to you.

### Notes

In making relational connections, there are two things going on: opportunity and risk.

Taking the risk means letting someone know how you feel about them.

What to do when a relationship hits a speed bump:

1. Show a need.

   God talks about his needs and takes massive risks.

2. Normalize speed bumps.

   Common speed bumps:

   - Miscommunication
   - Innocent triggering
   - Learning curve
   - Character flaw

   How to address speed bumps:

   - Talk about it.
     Choose a good time.

- Banish shame.

There is no shame in talking about a need, problem, hurt, or failure.

- Persevere.

How far can this relationship go? There is no limit.

"Now to him who is able to do immeasurably more than all we ask or imagine, according to his power that is at work within us, to him be glory in the church and in Christ Jesus throughout all generations, for ever and ever! Amen" (Ephesians 3:20–21).

Go deeper by talking about your:

| | |
|---|---|
| 1. Values | 5. Past |
| 2. Emotions | 6. Quirks |
| 3. Competencies | 7. Issues—your losses and injuries |
| 4. Preferences | 8. Yourselves |

Never settle. God wants you to keep working, keep trying, keep growing, keep pursuing.

**Group Discussion** (10 minutes)

Take a few minutes to talk about what you just watched.

1. What part of the teaching had the most impact on you?

*Take a Risk*

2. Moving into a relationship assumes that you are ready, the other person is ready, and you feel you have a green light to take the next step in moving beyond boundaries. In other words, you're ready to take a relational risk. Risk is an accelerant to intimacy and an essential step in building or rebuilding trust.

   The Bible includes several examples of risk-taking communication — statements that express vulnerability, need, and a desire for connection. Go around the group and have a different person read aloud the three passages below (pages 137–138). As the verses are read, underline any words or phrases that stand out to you. You may wish to read through the list twice to give everyone time to listen and respond.

   **God**
   How can I give you up, Ephraim? How can I hand you over, Israel? How can I treat you like Admah? How can I make you like Zeboyim? My heart is changed within me; all my compassion is aroused. *Hosea 11:8*

137

**Jesus**
Jerusalem, Jerusalem, you who kill the prophets and stone those sent to you, how often I have longed to gather your children together, as a hen gathers her chicks under her wings, and you were not willing.    *Matthew 23:37*

**The apostle Paul**
Oh, dear Corinthian friends! We have spoken honestly with you, and our hearts are open to you. There is no lack of love on our part, but you have withheld your love from us. I am asking you to respond as if you were my own children. Open your hearts to us!
*2 Corinthians 6:11–13 NLT*

- How would you describe the way these speakers engage in risk-taking communication?

- How do these verses impact you?

**Individual Activity:** **First-Risk Statements and Responses**
(7 minutes)

Complete this activity on your own.

The first risk you take in a relationship should be more about the present than the long-ago past. That is, it needs to be one of those "in the moment" risks that have to do with you and the other person—a problem, an event, or a pattern you are concerned about that the other person can readily understand and identify with, something you both know goes on between the two of you and perhaps has even happened in the recent past. A vulnerable statement then needs a vulnerable response—some expression of empathy, interest, assurance, or understanding—that conveys that the other person is on your side and that the risk was worth it.

1. Read through the three examples of first-risk statements and responses on the chart on page 140. Note how the first-risk statements focus on a present or recent event and express vulnerability. Also note how the responses express empathy and vulnerability.

2. Using the examples you read as a reference, write your own idea of what a vulnerable response might be to the next three statements on the chart.

3. In the last row on the chart, write a first-risk statement you could make in one of your current relationships and the kind of response you would hope to receive from the other person.

| VULNERABLE FIRST-RISK STATEMENTS | VULNERABLE RESPONSES |
|---|---|
| I got scared after we talked that you would distance yourself from me. | I know you were afraid I might pull away from you, but the opposite happened. After we talked, I felt a lot better about us and closer to you. |
| When I saw all the guys looking at you at the party, I got a little insecure. | I'm flattered that you thought other guys noticed me, but you don't have to worry about us. |
| I really messed up in our conversation yesterday; I made it more about me than about us. | When you made the conversation all about you, it wasn't fun. But it helps that you recognized it without me saying anything. That means a lot. |
| When you got angry and critical over the kids, it pushed me away as it did in the bad old days. | |
| I had a really bad day at work. Sorry to be such a downer tonight. | |
| I missed you this week and thought about you a lot. | |
| A vulnerable first-risk statement I could make ... | A vulnerable response I would hope to receive ... |

140

**Group Discussion** (19 minutes)

## First-Risk Statements and Responses

1. Briefly share some of the responses you wrote down for the three statements on the chart. What do you notice about each other's responses?

2. If you feel comfortable, share the first-risk statement (but not the response) you wrote on the last line of the chart. Next, allow the other members of the group to offer their ideas of what a vulnerable response to your statement might be. Finally, share the response you wrote on the chart. What do all of you observe about how the responses are similar to or different from each other?

## Deal with Speed Bumps

3. On the video, John talked about four common speed bumps that happen in relationships:

   *Miscommunication:* The other person doesn't understand what's going on with you, and the vulnerability-response cycle doesn't go well.

   *Innocent triggering:* The other person accidentally says or does something that triggers in you an old hurt from the past.

   *Learning curve:* Both of you have different styles and different preferences and it takes time to learn the particulars of the other person.

   *Character flaw:* This is a sign that something might be wrong—the other person is controlling, self-absorbed, deceptive, etc. If you raise the issue and the person owns it and works toward change, you've dealt with a speed bump. If they don't, it's more than a speed bump and could jeopardize the relationship.

- In your relationships overall, which speed bump would you say you have to deal with most often? If you can think of one, briefly share an example of this kind of speed bump.

- How do you typically respond to the speed bumps you deal with most often? For example, do you tend to overlook them and hope they'll go away? Address them directly and promptly? Overreact to them?

*Go Deeper*

4. Briefly discuss what you've learned and experienced together throughout this curriculum. What would you say is the most important thing you learned about relationships? How have you or your relationships been impacted by what you learned?

5. How would you characterize the differences in the ways you interact with and companion each other now compared to the beginning of the curriculum?

6. Describe the relational high points you experienced within the group. What moments stand out as some of the group's most loving, caring, or connected experiences?

7. What hopes do you have for the relationships in this group? Or, how do you hope to stretch yourself—to move beyond boundaries—for closer connections to other members of the group?

**Individual Activity: What I Want to Remember** (2 minutes)

Complete this activity on your own.

1. Briefly review the outline and any notes you took.
2. In the space below, write down the most significant thing you gained in this session—from the teaching, activities, or discussions.

   *What I want to remember from this session ...*

## Closing Prayer

Close your time together with prayer.

## SESSION 6 PERSONAL STUDY

### Read and Learn

Read chapters 19–21 of *Beyond Boundaries*. Use the space below to note any insights or questions you might have.

### Study and Reflect

1. How would you describe your risk style? Are you risk-averse, risk-neutral or risk-loving? Circle the number on the continuums below (pages 144–145) that best describe your response.

*Risk in general*

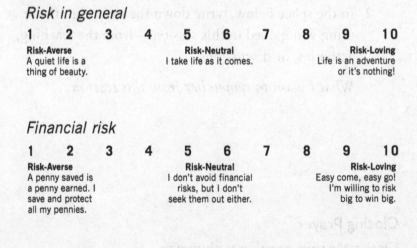

| 1 | 2 | 3 | 4 | 5 | 6 | 7 | 8 | 9 | 10 |
|---|---|---|---|---|---|---|---|---|----|

Risk-Averse
A quiet life is a thing of beauty.

Risk-Neutral
I take life as it comes.

Risk-Loving
Life is an adventure or it's nothing!

*Financial risk*

| 1 | 2 | 3 | 4 | 5 | 6 | 7 | 8 | 9 | 10 |
|---|---|---|---|---|---|---|---|---|----|

Risk-Averse
A penny saved is a penny earned. I save and protect all my pennies.

Risk-Neutral
I don't avoid financial risks, but I don't seek them out either.

Risk-Loving
Easy come, easy go! I'm willing to risk big to win big.

## Intellectual risk

1   2   3   4   5   6   7   8   9   10

**Risk-Averse**
I prefer to read, watch, or listen to things that reinforce and deepen my existing views.

**Risk-Neutral**
I don't have a preference about reading, watching, or listening to things that support or challenge my existing views.

**Risk-Loving**
I prefer to read, watch, or listen to things that challenge and expand my existing views.

## Physical risk

1   2   3   4   5   6   7   8   9   10

**Risk-Averse**
Why do you think God made seatbelts?

**Risk-Neutral**
Who knows! (Or cares?)

**Risk-Loving**
Why do you think God made bungee cords?

## Relational risk

1   2   3   4   5   6   7   8   9   10

**Risk-Averse**
I'm guarded and rarely share my heart with others.

**Risk-Neutral**
I'm not guarded, but I'm not wide open either.

**Risk-Loving**
I'm wide open and often share my heart with others.

Based on your responses, how would you describe your overall risk style?

How does your relational risk style compare with your risk styles in other areas? What do you think accounts for the similarities or differences?

2. Risk is always a little scary or it wouldn't be risk. But an investment in healthy relational risk also has the potential to yield great returns. Instead of focusing on the scary part, what hopes and dreams are you aware of when you allow yourself to focus on the "returns"—the good things that your relational risks could bring?

3. On the video, John presented three skills for dealing with speed bumps:

   *Talk about it:* Be willing to say, "This is a problem."

   *Banish shame:* When the other person exposes his/her heart—about questions, failures, and needs—extend grace. No one should feel judged, condemned, or shamed for bringing up a problem, sharing a need, or acknowledging vulnerability.

   *Persevere:* Good relationships take work. Be willing to do the right relational things over and over again even when you don't feel close.

   Of the three skills, which is the hardest for you to practice in your relationships? What makes this skill especially difficult for you?

   *Talk about it.* Read "Talk about Talking" on page 148 and then complete the following chart. Identify three relationships from different areas of your life (family, friends, colleagues, etc.) and write their names on the chart. Using the examples you just read as a reference, write a brief statement for each person that addresses a speed bump-level concern you have in that relationship.

| NAME | HOW I CAN TALK ABOUT TALKING IN THIS RELATIONSHIP |
|---|---|
|  |  |
|  |  |
|  |  |

## TALK ABOUT TALKING

People who want to improve a relationship often talk about talking. That is, they bring up what happened and what went wrong in their experience and come up with solutions. Here are some examples:

- Remember when I said I need space and listening, not solutions and homework assignments? It happened again; let's fix this.

- I don't want to sound childish, but I've been trying to be more open about the job problem, and it still feels as if you want just good news from me about work. I really need you to hang in there with me.

- It feels as if you're impatient with me when I go to a deeper level now, as if I ought to have my act together. That's hard for me; are you really feeling that way?

- When I brought up the problems I have with my dad, you lost eye contact and started talking about something else. This is really important for me; are you okay with all this? Is there a way I can do this differently, or do you not want me to talk about this with you?

Be a team player with the person. In responding, you must have no hint of judgment or a critical spirit. You are forging a way to connect.... You want to recruit the person to vulnerable language, to solve the glitch and move on.

*Beyond Boundaries*, pages 254–255

*Banish shame.* Exposing your heart in the relationship needs to be welcomed, not shamed. Pick one of the names you wrote on the chart on page 147 and write it below.

Now write one or two welcoming statements you might say to extend grace to this person the next time he/she takes a risk with you. For example, "Thanks for letting me know how you feel. That would be hard for me too. Let's talk it through."

*Persevere.* Read "Persevere ... to a Point" on pages 150–151. Then respond to the questions below.

What is your perseverance tendency in relationships? Place an X on the continuum below to indicate your response.

| | |
|---|---|
| In my difficult relationships, I almost always give up too soon. | In my difficult relationships, I almost always persevere too long. |

In which of your relationships do you feel God may be inviting you to persevere? In which might you need to get support or make changes? What do you need from God and/or the other person(s) that would help you to take next steps?

## PERSEVERE ... TO A POINT

Things won't always feel close, and there will be disconnects, but don't give up too quickly. Be willing to persevere—even if you don't feel close or hopeful. Get back on the horse again. Great relationships that last a long time always have some periods in which the individuals feel alienated from each other but decide to face each other again and work out the problem. Perseverance means doing the right relational things even when there is no real passion behind it. It's sticking to God's deep values of love, grace, honesty, ownership, and stewardship....

But even perseverance has its limits. You can't persevere just by trying harder over and over again. There are always two things to consider when you persevere in working through vulnerability speed bumps as you seek to move beyond your protective boundaries:

1. *Be energized from the outside.* If things aren't working well, you must not do this alone. It is not possible to continue taking risks when you are in isolation from everyone but the person you are trying to connect with. Make sure you are getting encouragement and support from others.

2. *Change what needs to be changed.* If you are continually experiencing withdrawal, blame, irresponsibility, or deception on the other end of the relationship, it's no character virtue to keep taking risks that aren't working. It's been said that insanity is doing the same thing over and over again and expecting a different result. That's a problem.

So give the person, yourself, and the relationship lots of time and room to make mistakes in vulnerability. As you continue to deal with the obstacles to intimacy, they will be less discouraging over time, and you will simply experience them as a normal part of relational life.

*Beyond Boundaries*, pages 256–258

4. Making the effort to develop intimacy is important not only for your connections but for your entire life. You were meant to be free, not careful; open about yourself, not closed down; capable of deep attachments, not disconnected. You were designed to follow love and live in love, becoming like the One who embodies love itself (1 John 4:16). And you can rely on the promise that God is already at work to bring this about — in you and in your relationships:

> Now all glory to God, who is able, through his mighty power at work within us, to accomplish infinitely more than we might ask or think. Glory to him in the church and in Christ Jesus through all generations forever and ever! Amen. *Ephesians 3:20–21 NLT*

What do you long for God to do for you? What is the "infinitely more" you want his power to accomplish in you?

What is the "infinitely more" you want God's power to accomplish in your relationships?

151

## Guided Prayer

*God, thank you for inviting me to take relational risks and for helping me to become more like you when I do.*

*The more I learn about relationships, the more I realize how much I need to grow and change. Please change my heart, especially ...*

*I want to have deep connections and experience the kind of relationships I was made for, but I also have wounds and unhealthy patterns that always seem to get in my way. Please heal me of ...*

*I entrust to you the difficult relationships I'm struggling with ...*

*I ask for the power and the desire to take the relational risks you are inviting me to take, especially ...*

*God, thank you for your risky, way-beyond-boundaries love for me. Amen.*

# Beyond Boundaries

## Learning to Trust Again in Relationships

*Dr. John Townsend*

How do you know you're ready to trust again ... and what does it take to be ready?

Painful relationships violate our trust, causing us to close our hearts. But to experience the freedom and love God designed us for, we eventually have to take another risk.

In this breakthrough book, bestselling author Dr. John Townsend takes you beyond the pain of the past to discover how to re-enter a life of intimate relationships. Whether you're trying to restore a current relationship or begin a new one, Townsend gives practical tools for establishing trust and finding the intimacy you long for.

*Beyond Boundaries* will help you reinstate closeness with someone who broke your trust; discern when true change has occurred; reestablish appropriate connections in strained relationships; create a safe environment that helps you trust; and restore former relationships to a healthy dynamic.

You can move past relational pain to trust again.

*Beyond Boundaries* will show you how.

# Boundaries

## When To Say Yes, When to Say No to Take Control of Your Life

*Dr. Henry Cloud and Dr. John Townsend with Lisa Guest*

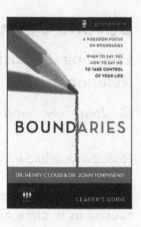

- Do you have trouble saying no?
- Can you set limits and still be a loving person?
- Are you in control of your life?
- What are legitimate boundaries?
- Do people take advantage of you?
- How do you answer someone who wants your time, love, energy, and money?

Drs. Henry Cloud and John Townsend offer biblically based answers to these tough questions as they show us how to set healthy boundaries with our parents, our spouses, our children, our friends, our coworkers, and even ourselves. Designed for use with the *Boundaries Participant's Guide*, this compelling nine-part video resource helps us define and maintain the clear personal boundaries that are essential to a healthy and balanced life.

**Sessions Include:**
1. What Is a Boundary?
2. Understanding Boundaries
3. The Laws of Boundaries, Part 1
4. The Laws of Boundaries, Part 2
5. Myths about Boundaries
6. Boundary Conflicts, Part 1
7. Boundary Conflicts, Part 2
8. Boundary Successes, Part 1
9. Boundary Successes, Part 2

*Available in stores and online!*

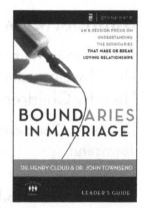

# Making Your Small Group Work

*Henry Cloud, Bill Donahue, and John Townsend*

In *Making Your Small Group Work*, Henry Cloud, Bill Donahue, and John Townsend provide four sixty-minute sessions to train leaders and group members in the foundational values and practices of becoming a life-changing community. These sixty-minute sessions are the foundations of small groups that include teaching by the authors, creative segments, and activities and discussion time.

The group has the chance to review and learn new group life techniques over the course of four in-depth sessions:

- Session 1 provides a foundational experience that helps group members get excited about the adventure and life-changing power of small group life.
- Session 2 focuses on introducing values, ground rules, and logistical issues to deepen relationships.
- Session 3 unpacks each of the five key values through in-depth teaching and practical examples.
- Session 4 transitions the group to running on its own, using a variety of exercises to help the group clarify what their focus will be, and what they want to do in their next meeting.

*Making Your Small Group Work* helps leaders to create strong relationships and promote the kind of in-depth discussion that will help everyone grow in their spirituality.

Designed for use with the *Making Your Small Group Work Participant's Guide*.

*Available in stores and online!*